THE ARROW SEASIDE COMPANION

KU-111-927

BY THE SAME AUTHOR

The Modern Sea Angler
A Complete Guide to Sea Fishing
Sea Fishing in South Devon
Sea Fishing in Cornwall
Sea Fishing in Dorset
Sea Fishing in North Devon and Somerset
Sea Fishing in Hampshire and the Isle of Wight
Sea Fishing in Sussex
Sea Fishing in Kent
Fishing for Bass

HUGH STOKER

The Arrow Seaside Companion

Illustrated by
**DENNIS AND BARBARA YOUNG
AND BY HUGH STOKER**

ARROW BOOKS

ARROW BOOKS LTD

178–202 Great Portland Street, London W1

AN IMPRINT OF THE   HUTCHINSON GROUP

London Melbourne Sydney
Auckland Bombay Toronto
Johannesburg New York

First published 1956 by
Hutchinson & Co. (*Publishers*) Ltd.
as *The Seaside Pocket Companion*

Arrow edition, completely revised and with
new material added, first published 1966

*For copyright reasons this book may not be
issued to the public on loan or otherwise
except in its original soft cover*

Revised edition © Hugh Stoker 1966

*Made and printed in Great Britain
by The Anchor Press, Ltd.,
Tiptree, Essex*

TO

MY MOTHER

and

to the memory of the menfolk of her family, crew of the lugger Reform, *of Deal, who lost their lives on the morning of 16th January, 1871,*

while attempting to rescue the crew of a vessel in distress on the Goodwin Sands

Contents

FISHING SECTION

Illustrations

Author's Note

Certain parts of this book have appeared in abbreviated form as magazine articles, and the customary acknowledgements are accordingly made to the editors of the following publications: *Angling Times, Collins' Young Elizabethan, Cycling,* and *Out of Doors*.

I would also like to thank the undermentioned firms and societies for their willing assistance in the matter of technical information and illustrations: The Royal Life Saving Society; The Royal National Lifeboat Institution; Messrs. Allcock & Company, Limited, of Redditch; The British Trawlers' Federation; The Esso Petroleum Company, Limited; The Fishmongers' Company; and Frederick Warne & Co. Ltd., publishers of *Birds of the British Isles*, in which appear the coloured illustrations by Archibald Thorburn used in preparing the drawings of sea birds.

THE LURE OF THE ROCK POOLS 1
PRAWNING, LOBSTERING AND CRABBING.

I started writing the rough draft of this book one hot July afternoon, while sitting on the beach waiting for the tide to go out. At my side—well to leeward!—lay my prawning nets, already baited with pieces of over-ripe kipper. On my shoulder was slung an old gas-mask haversack, which during the next few hours I hoped to fill with a mixed bag of prawns, lobsters and edible crabs.

Several other rock-pool enthusiasts were dotted about on the beach nearby; some of them holidaymakers, but the majority local inhabitants like myself. There were women as well as men, girls as well as boys; their ages ranging from about seven years to nearly seventy. The managing director of a well-known paint firm was there with his drop nets, determined to catch his supper. The village postmaster and his wife, filled with the same stern resolve, were busily baiting up their nets with some old rabbits' guts. A little farther away I also recognised a farmer acquaintance of mine—a veritable enthusiast among enthusiasts. He had driven nearly fifty miles from his farm in Wiltshire just to enjoy this one low spring tide, and I was not at all surprised to see that he and his son were already prospecting close to the water's edge, carrying their dozen baited nets between them.

First off the mark that afternoon, however, was Doctor J——, who had left his patients to fend for themselves while he indulged in his favourite pastime. The doctor is a hand netter, and long before the tide had dropped enough to allow the rest of us to use our bait nets he was wading about in the nearest rock pools, often with only his round, jovial face, and battered old panama hat, showing above water. We on the beach watched him with interest to see what the sport was like that day, and were encouraged by the fact that he seemed to be doing pretty well. On one occasion, in fact, he held up for our inspection a 'girt gran'fer' of a prawn that must have been nearly four inches long.

This hand netting is easily the cheapest method of catching prawns, as the only equipment required is a simple, long-handled net which may be bought very reasonably at most seaside tackle shops in the West country. The best 'prawning counties' are Dorset, Devon, Cornwall and North Somerset, and many different sorts of net are to be seen in use around these coasts, each district favouring a certain type, as local conditions dictate. In places where eel grass grows in abundance I have seen the ordinary broad, wooden-boomed shrimping net used with success. The majority of districts, however, favour either a round or slightly pear-shaped frame made of stout galvanised metal. In West Dorset we prefer a pear-shaped frame that is tilted slightly upwards from the handle, considering it the best shape for catching prawns among seaweed-covered recesses in the rocks, where they often lurk between the tides. The technique that brings the best results with this type of net consists, very briefly, of a forward underwater thrust of the net beneath the weed festooning the boulders, or into holes in the rock ; followed immediately by a quick upwards and backwards scraping movement of the net.

It will be seen that this method entails subjecting the net to some rough treatment, and because of this constant scraping of the galvanised frame against the rock the netting is not braided directly on to it. Instead, it is suspended from a copper wire attached to the frame by a series of copper nipples. There are, it is true, some cheap nets on the market which have the netting lashed to the frame with twine, but they are little better than toys, and are never used by the serious prawner.

As the use of a hand net necessitates wading, often up to the shoulders, one should always be equipped with swimming-trunks and a pair of old canvas shoes. Rope soles are safer than rubber ones on wet rock, although even rope will slip on the treacherous green silk weed. Professional prawners (there *are* such people) often wear hob-nailed boots, reserved specially for the job.

Naturally, it is necessary to carry something to put the catch in, and the most favoured receptacle is a cloth bag, fitted with a strong tape so that it can be slung over the shoulder. The neck of the bag should be just large enough to allow the prawns—and possibly a lobster or two—to be thrust into it without fumbling. A flap, which can be buttoned over the opening, is helpful when one is wading deep,

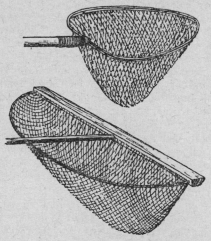

Prawn or shrimping nets: (*above*) pear-shaped frame for use among rock pools, (*below*) the boomed type shrimping net

as it will prevent those prawns already caught from swimming out of the bag. In windy weather a stone placed inside the bag will prevent it from blowing about and spilling its contents.

The advantages of the hand net are that it requires no bait; the net itself is light to carry, and with it prawns can usually be caught in good numbers under any reasonable weather conditions. The main disadvantage lies in the fact that one has to wade about in the water for long periods at a time; no hardship, it is true, on a warm, sunny day, but a chilly business when there is a keen east wind blowing. Also, the chances of the beginner catching a lobster with a hand net are rather remote, although it can be done by first enticing the lobster out of its rock lair with a piece of bait tied to one end of a length of string.

As a rule, however, the drop net, or bait net as it is also called, is the tackle most popular among those who wish to catch lobsters and edible crabs as well as prawns. It consists of a circular, bag-shaped net attached to a round metal hoop; the hoop in turn being attached to a length of rope made buoyant by two pieces of cork (*see* illustration). One piece of cork is fastened to that end of the rope nearest the hoop, and the other is knotted to the end held by the prawner. This second piece of cork is purely a precautionary measure, so that the end of the rope can be found again should it happen to fall into the water. Unlike the hand net, the drop net needs to be baited, and for this purpose lengths of tarred twine are stretched across the hoop in pairs in the form of a cross. The bait, usually a piece of fish or rabbit flesh, is slipped between the strands of twine, and then held firmly in place by a small running noose. The net is then dropped into the rock pool and allowed to remain there for a minute or two, or considerably longer if there is any chance of a lobster being in the vicinity. After making sure that the rope is taut, the net is hauled in again as quickly and steadily as possible, hand over hand. Any prawns which may have been caught will be leaping about in the bottom of the net, and after they have been transferred to the 'catch-bag' the net is dropped back into the water.

By this time the bait will have been savoured by prawns some distance away, and, as they swim to investigate, the catches should grow larger and larger. When, after a dozen or more drops, they gradually begin to fall off again, that is the time to move on and try another rock pool; or another part of the same pool if it covers a large area. It is a point worth remembering, though, that the deeper the pool, and the closer one can keep to the low-tide line, the larger will be the prawns which one catches.

Most drop-net prawners declare that good results are most likely to be obtained on days when the water is 'cloudy', and even more so at dusk or after dark. A consoling factor on days when the water in the pools is very clear, however, is that although the prawns may be shy, it is possible to gaze into the furthest depths of a veritable submarine wonderland and watch the myriads of strange little creatures which inhabit it—the bullheads and chubby-faced blennies, the multicoloured anemones, and, most amazing of all, the 'sea cu-

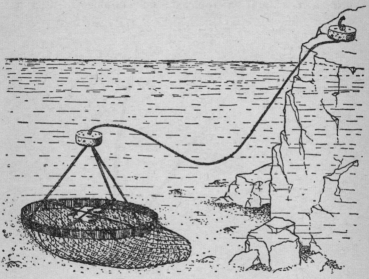

How to use the drop net

cumber', that evades its foes by spinning a mass of elastic threads as it hurries away, so that its pursuer becomes hopelessly entangled in them and is forced to abandon the chase. Then there are the crabs, dozens of them, nearly all of them worthless as food, yet extremely interested in your bait. You begin to realise, then, why your bait seems to disappear so quickly.

Drop-netting from rocks or a sea-eroded harbour wall on the open coast also offers a good chance of catching a lobster. For lobsters the best bait of all is a piece of kipper, and the most likely places are to be found well out among the furthest rocks, in those pools which never hold less than three or four feet of water, even at low spring tides. Experience has shown that when the small crabs hold aloof from the bait it is often a sign that there is a lobster in the vicinity.

Except for its coral pink 'whiskers', the lobster is slate-blue in its natural environment; only turning red after it

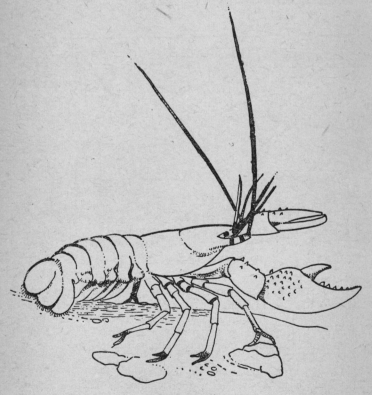

Lobster crawling

has been caught and boiled. The first indication that one is at hand will, in all probability, be a glimpse of those pink whiskers appearing slowly from its weed-curtained lair. There is something about the sight that makes one quite breathless with excitement.

The lobster is an extremely cautious creature, and the greatest care and skill are necessary to land one successfully. Although its normal mode of progress is a slow forwards crawl, it can retreat in a flash by doubling its spade-like tail quickly beneath its body. This sends it shooting backwards, and it is usually a long time before a scared lobster manages to get over its fright and ventures out into the open again.

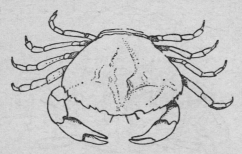

The edible crab

Consequently, before there is a reasonable chance of catching a lobster in a drop net it must be allowed to crawl right up to the bait, and its tail must be inside the rim of the metal hoop. As an adult lobster has a long body, and can also reach for the bait with its claws from a distance of several inches, it is obvious that a large net is essential. One with a diameter of less than two feet is almost useless for lobstering, unless—and this requires considerable skill—a hand net can be slid down into the water unnoticed by the lobster, and positioned so that, as soon as it is scared by the hauling in of the drop net, it shoots backwards into the hand net.

The edible crab is much more easy to catch than the lobster, being less timid and slower in its movements. Quite often, in fact, a crab will make no attempt at all to escape from the net when it is hauled out of the water, and on closer examination will be found to be still greedily clasping the bait with its claws.

Most people are familiar with the appearance of the edible crab; for it is usually displayed prominently on fishmongers' stalls. Unlike the lobster, it does not change colour to any marked extent when boiled, and may be recognised quite easily by its round, rather flat-topped carapace, which is somewhat like a large mince pie in colour and shape. In fact, it really does look good enough to eat.

Spider crab

Most other rock-pool crabs, on the other hand, do not look nearly so appetising; they are smaller than the full-grown edible crab, and in the majority of cases their shells range in colour from olive green to a sort of seaweed-brown. An exception is the spider crab, which attains quite a considerable size, is dark red in colour, and on some coasts is often caught in the drop net. There is, however, no risk of confusing it with the edible crab, as its shell is more pear-shaped, and covered with numerous spines and nodules. Indeed, on some parts of the coast it is known as the thorn-back. Contrary to common belief, this rather unpleasant-looking crab is good to eat, and thousands find their way every year into the canning factories.

At very low spring tides it is also possible to haul lobsters and edible crabs out of their hiding-places among the rocks with a long-handled gaff. This method requires considerable skill, however, and an intimate knowledge of the rock pools. If you have no gaff with you, but happen to see a lobster go to ground in a rock fissure, the temptation to thrust a hand into the hole and drag its occupant out quickly by the tail can be very great. It is a temptation that should on all accounts be resisted, however. A large lobster possesses a claw that is powerful enough to crush a finger; whilst to meddle bare-handed with a crab in its lair can even prove fatal. The edible crab, when alarmed, will often raise itself up on tiptoe, as it were, and when this happens a person's hand can easily become trapped between the crab's carapace and the top of the rock fissure. Grisly tales—founded on fact—are related by longshoremen about people who found themselves held helpless in this manner on lonely stretches of coast, to be ultimately drowned when the tide came in again.

Boat Netting for Prawns, Lobsters and Crabs

With reasonably good sea conditions, and several drop nets, it is possible to make some really profitable hauls of prawns, lobsters and crabs when fishing from a boat. The technique is very similar to that employed in rock-pool fishing, except that the nets are dropped into the water some distance apart, leaving the corks at the end of each rope floating on the water to mark the spot. Naturally, when first using nets in this manner it is necessary to make quite sure that the corks are large enough to bear the weight of the rope, and that the rope itself is long enough to reach from the sea-bed to the surface. It is, in fact, a wise plan to have about a fathom of rope to spare, especially if the tide is rising.

Best results are usually obtained if the nets are dropped in sheltered water, as close as possible to the rocks. Small creeks and gullies, bordered by seaweed-covered rocks, are especially good places to try. The simplest method is to drop the nets about three fathoms apart in a more or less straight line, and then to row back gently to the first net and start hauling in again. Do not row close to the line of nets, though, or the sound of your oars may scare off a timid lobster. For the same reason, when approaching a net to haul it in, it is best to take two or three hard pulls at the oars, and then to drift the rest of the way to the floating cork. Boat netting is, in fact, best done by two people ; one rowing the boat, and the other standing in the bows in readiness to grab the cork. It is most important that the rope should be hauled in straight away, without any preliminary fumbling.

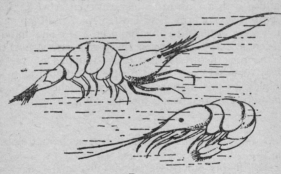

Prawns

Boat netting for prawns, lobsters and crabs is essentially a calm weather job, for it is invariably carried on close inshore, and among rocks. Even if the day is fine and windless it can be a risky pastime if there is anything like a swell running. Under such conditions, the keen drop netter would be well advised to curb his enthusiasm and stick to the rock pools.

EXAMINING THE CATCH

People nowadays have become so used to buying all their food in shops that when they have caught several quarts of prawns there are quite a number who fear there must be a snag somewhere. Remembering tales of people becoming seriously ill through eating contaminated shell-fish, they begin to have grave doubts as to the wisdom of eating what they have just caught. If only they knew how much more wholesome their prawns were than those ready-cooked ones on sale in the shops!

Nevertheless, the catch is carefully examined, and when some of the larger prawns are found to have a discoloured swelling on one side of the head they are usually thrown away in the belief that they harbour some fearful malignant growth. Actually, these swollen-faced prawns—popularly known as 'ear-achers'—are quite wholesome, the swelling being due to a small parasitic creature that is innocuous to human beings, and which is, in any case, removed with the head of the prawn when it is shelled.

Round about May and June, when the prawning season really begins, one will come across many prawns carrying clusters of tiny globules between their swimming legs. These are females with their eggs, and are usually referred to as being 'in berry'. Female lobsters also carry their eggs in a somewhat similar manner, but when caught they should, by law, be returned to the water so that they may complete their maternal duties. Similarly, young lobsters measuring less than nine inches from head-spike to tail-tip should be returned so that they may have an opportunity of growing into a really worthwhile meal in a few years' time.

MAKING YOUR OWN NETS

As previously mentioned, a hand net is not expensive to buy, and little would be gained by trying to make your own. Drop nets, however, are a different proposition. At the time of writing, a single net, fitted to a 24-inch-diameter hoop, costs upwards of 30s. when bought at a shop—and few really keen drop netters are content to work with only one net. In fact half a dozen is the usual number when prawning or lobstering from the rocks, and a dozen or more when a small boat is being used.

It is, however, a simple enough matter to make a perfectly satisfactory drop net at home; the cost being only about a tenth of the shop-bought article. The things required to carry out the job are an old metal hoop, some good quality $\frac{1}{4}$ in. or $\frac{1}{3}$ in. square-mesh netting, about 7 or 8 yards of thin rope, some tarred twine, and two large pieces of cork, approximately 4 in. in diameter and 2 in thick. The length of the piece of netting should be equal to the circumference of the hoop, and the width about two-thirds the length.

Having collected your materials, the first thing to do is to take the hoop and bind one of the long edges of the netting to it with the tarred twine, passing the twine round the hoop, and through about every fifth mesh of the net. It is a good plan to secure every tenth turn of the twine with a knot, so that if at any time the twine should fray through the whole job will not immediately come unravelled. When you have finished binding the netting to the hoop it should be hanging down neatly like a circular curtain, as in Figure 1.

Now comes the only tricky part—you have to transform this open-ended circle of netting into a pouch-shaped bag. To do this it is necessary to trim away with a pair of sharp scissors the two ends of the circle of netting, so that a large wedge-shaped gap is formed, similar in shape to that shown in Figure 2. When cutting the netting you will be well advised to snip through one mesh at a time, taking care not to cut too near the knots joining the netting. It is essential that good quality netting be used, with properly made knots which will not slip.

Having cut out the wedge of netting, the next task is to draw the severed edges together and join them by running twine through the meshes. This job should be done carefully, and the twine knotted after joining each pair of meshes. When you have finished the edges, lace up the bottom of the net by the same method. You will then have a pouch-shaped net, as shown in Figure 3.

Next take some more tarred twine and tie two strands across the top of the hoop at right angles to one another,

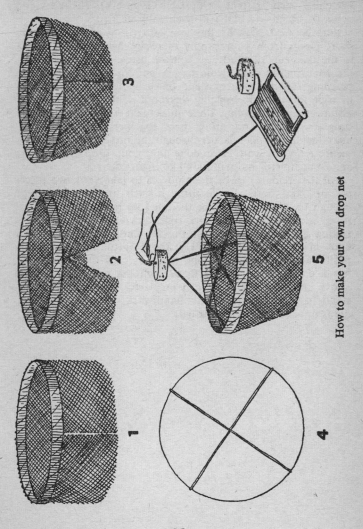

How to make your own drop net

stretching each as tight as possible (Figure 4). These are the cords to which the bait will eventually be tied.

For the next part of the job you will need to cut three short pieces from your supply of rope, each equal in length to the diameter of the hoop you are using. Whip the ends of the rope tightly with twine to prevent the strands from un-ravelling. Then attach one end of each of these three pieces of rope to the hoop, spacing them out so that they are equal distances apart. Having done this, make small loops in the three free ends, and bring them together. Now take your main length of rope, pass it through the three loops, and tie it securely. When you have done this your drop net will be almost complete, and will look like Figure 5.

All that remains to be done now is to take your two pieces of cork and bore a hole through each of them just large enough to allow them to be threaded on to the long piece of rope. Slide one piece of cork right down the rope until it is resting against the knots at the far end. Then tie another knot in the rope immediately above it to hold it in that position. Now slip the second piece of cork on to the rope, but keep it at the end farthest from the net, tying a knot above and below it to hold it in place. After that you may stand back and admire your handiwork, because your drop net is finished and ready for use.

The following are a few of the many ways of preparing prawns, lobsters and crabs for the table.

PRAWNS

Immediately upon returning home from a prawning expedition the catch should be thoroughly washed. This may be done by placing the prawns in a vessel half filled with water and allowing them to swim around in it for a while. If the vessel is a shallow one some sort of a lid should be placed over it, as prawns are quite capable of leaping out of the water.

To Boil Prawns. First bring to the boil a panful of water, in which has been dissolved a handful of salt for every quart of water. Drop the prawns into the pan and keep the water boiling gently for about seven minutes, by which time the prawns will have turned a pinkish-red. Strain off the water and allow the prawns to cool before serving. When eating prawns the heads and tails are pinched off with the finger and thumb, whereupon—with freshly cooked prawns, at any rate—the rest of the shell falls away from the flesh quite easily.

Fried Prawns. With 4 oz. of flour, 6 oz. of milk, 1 egg, and a pinch of pepper and salt, mix up a batter and allow to stand. Meanwhile, boil a quantity of prawns as described above and shell when cool. Then melt some lard in a frying-pan, and, dipping the prawns one by one in the batter, transfer them quickly into the boiling fat and fry until a golden brown. Serve on hot buttered toast.

Potted Prawns. Boil the prawns, and when cool remove their heads, tails and shell. To every half-pint of prawns thus prepared allow 2 oz. of butter, a little ground mace and cayenne

27

pepper, and a separate 1 oz. of butter. Put the 2 oz. of butter into an enamel saucepan, and melt over a low flame. Add the prawns, mace and pepper, and continue to heat gently without allowing the butter to boil. When the prawns have been thoroughly warmed, pour the mixture into glass pots to within a quarter of an inch of the top. Allow to cool, and then make the jars air-tight by adding clarified butter. Cover up the jars when the butter has cooled.

LOBSTERS

To Boil a Lobster. Tie the claws of the lobster with string and wash it thoroughly under a running tap. Meanwhile, half fill a *very large* saucepan with salty water and bring thoroughly to the boil. Plunge the lobster in *head first*. If these instructions are carried out the lobster's end will be swift and sure. As soon as the lobster is in the pot, reduce the amount of heat and allow the water to simmer gently for about twenty minutes, or slightly longer if the lobster is a large one. Then remove the lobster and plunge it into cold water.

Incidentally, lobsters do *not* scream when boiled. The shrill whistling sound which is sometimes heard emanating from the pot is caused by air escaping through crevices in the lobster's shell.

There is another method of boiling lobsters which is supposed to be perfectly painless, and is, in fact, recommended by the R.S.P.C.A. in a special pamphlet published by them on the subject. Strangely enough, it consists of placing the lobster in cold water and very gradually raising the temperature. The warmth penetrates the shell slowly, destroying the nervous system gradually and painlessly, so that the lobster dies before the water has become more than tepid. This may be hard to believe, but anyone who puts it to the test will never go back to the old, heartless method of plunging a lobster straight into boiling water. Further details are given later on in this chapter, in the section dealing with crabs, which may also be cooked in this way. Remember, though, those two important points, place the lobster in *cold* water, and warm *slowly*.

Lobster Mayonnaise

> 1 fair-sized lobster ; 2 hard-boiled eggs ;
> 2 fresh lettuces ; Mayonnaise dressing.

Boil the lobster and, when cool, crack the shell and remove the meat as whole as possible. Cut up the meat into small cubes, sprinkling each with a trace of salt, pepper and vinegar. Spread a layer of crisp lettuce leaves at the bottom of the salad bowl, then a layer of lobster meat, and so on, alternately, until all the lobster and lettuce have been used. Pour mayonnaise dressing over the top, and garnish with boiled prawns and sliced egg.

CRABS

To Boil a Crab. Crabs should be boiled in salty water in the same way as lobsters, the time allowed for cooking ranging from fifteen to twenty minutes, according to size. Often crabs are killed by stabbing before being consigned to the cooking-pot, owing to their habit of shedding their claws when plunged into boiling water.

However, since the R.S.P.C.A. published their pamphlet on killing crabs and lobsters for the table I have made a point of following the instructions recommended by them. After placing the crab alive in a saucepan of cold water the temperature is slowly raised over a low heat. Without any apparent distress, the crab expires completely when the water reaches the 'luke-warm' stage. Then, and only then, is the heat turned on fully under the saucepan, and the water brought to the boil. The period of boiling varies with the size of the crab, but will normally be from 20 to 30 minutes. At the end of this time the crab should be plunged into cold water to stop the cooking process, which would otherwise continue for some time under the hot shell.

Extracting the meat of the cooked crab is regarded by

many people as being a rather complicated procedure; although it is, in fact, quite simple. Of course, a personal demonstration by someone who is an expert at the job is always best in matters of this sort, but the following is the generally recognised method. First of all, the claws and legs are removed, and the meat extracted from them by means of a pair of nut-crackers. After that, the shell, or carapace, is wrenched off, and the meat inside removed. The only inedible parts here are the gills; otherwise known as 'deaf-ears' or 'dead man's fingers'. They are greyish in colour, and do, in fact, look as much like small, flabby fingers as anything else. To eat them is supposed to be dangerous, and care should be taken to see that they are completely discarded.

Dressed Crab. An attractive way of serving crab meat is to mix it with vinegar, mustard, salt and a little pepper. The empty shell of the crab is then washed and dried, and the meat replaced in it before serving.

Crab Salad. Place the crab meat in the centre of a salad bowl, leaving the claws on top. Surround it with lettuce, sliced raw tomatoes, radishes, cucumber, etc.

Hot Crab. After removing the crab meat, wash and dry the empty shell. Mix the meat with a trace of nutmeg, salt, pepper, a small pat of butter or margarine, a few breadcrumbs, a teaspoonful of mustard, and two teaspoonfuls of vinegar. Pack the mixture into the shell, and cook in a moderate oven until lightly browned. Serve with hot toast.

No one who lives near a stretch of sheltered shore need ever starve, for a little scratching around with a rake or garden hoe at low tide will reveal a wide variety of edible shellfish. Most sought after, perhaps, among these offerings of the seashore is the cockle, which hides itself under the sand at low water. Its shell is thick and ribbed, and like other burrowing molluscs it possesses a muscular 'foot', by means of which it can dig its way into the sand in a matter of seconds.

Cockle

At high tide, when covered by water, it breathes and eats by means of two short tubes, situated at the end opposite its foot. Through one of these water and suspended food matter are taken in, while the other tube acts as an 'exhaust' for the water after it has been filtered through the gills and sieve-like digestive organs. Because of this method of feeding, the cockle—and many other types of shellfish—can become tainted when living in polluted water, and none should be gathered in the vicinity of sewage outfalls, or in the estuaries of rivers that are not thoroughly scoured by the tides. In any case, enquiries on this point should always be made locally before gathering shellfish on an unfamiliar shore.

Apart from the cockle, there are numerous other types of mollusc which may be gathered for the table. Among these are the Otter Clams, Gaper Clams (*Mya arenaria*), and the familiar, long, slaty-blue Razor Clams. The last-named are extremely popular as food in America, where several million dollars' worth are canned every year on the Pacific and New England coasts. In this country they are not appreciated as much as they should be.

Gaper and Razor Clams are generally found buried between the tide lines, the Gaper favouring a mixture of sand and mud, and the Razor Clam preferring clean sand. Their

Razor clam

presence is revealed by a slight depression in the surface; round in the case of the Gaper, while that of the Razor is slit-shaped. The latter molluscs are capable of burrowing at a very rapid rate, and digging them out can be an exasperating business for the beginner. A barbed, spear-shaped probe made from a piece of tough wire, is often used to drag them from their holes.

There can be few people who are not familiar with the whelk, so easily recognised by its large, spiral, cone-shaped shell. It is the vampire of the shellfish world, for it preys on other molluscs by drilling through their shells, afterwards

Whelk

sucking out their juiciest portions by means of a long, flexible snout, rather like a tiny elephant's trunk. Nevertheless, despite its unpleasant feeding habits it makes excellent eating, as those who have patronised the whelk stalls to be found at most large holiday resorts will know. Many who have a partiality for whelks will have no corresponding love of large seaside resorts, however, and with boat and drop-net it will often be possible to gather enough of these shellfish for their supper. Incidentally, it is an interesting point that, although the vast majority of whelk shells spiral towards the right, one occasionally happens upon a shell with a left-handed 'thread', as it were. According to one authority, the chances of making such a find are about one in a thousand.

Winkle

As familiar as the whelk is the winkle, a great favourite with the connoisseurs of shellfish. They are usually to be found where sand gives way to a more rocky type of coast, and at low tide may be gathered in enormous quantities around the edges of shallow pools, or low down on the sheltered side of the rocks. Despite their toothsome qualities, winkles (or peri-winkles, to give them their full name) are the victims of a certain amount of snobbishness, and rarely will the author of a cookery book deign to offer advice upon how to prepare them for the table. This grave injustice has been righted in the next chapter.

While on the subject of winkles, however, it might be as well to offer a brief warning. If you gather them in a bucket, make sure that something is placed firmly over the top when reaching home in order to keep them under control. It is surprising how far and fast a winkle can travel when it has a mind to, and nothing is more annoying than to have to pick several hundred off the walls and ceiling of a tastefully decorated room. If staying in somebody else's house one's popularity as a guest undergoes a sudden slump!

Mussels are another popular type of edible shellfish, and may be found on practically any stretch of coast that affords them suitable places where they can anchor their shells. As is the case with other types of mollusc, however, great care must be taken in seeing that those gathered for human consumption come from water that is not contaminated in any way, and it is an offence to offer for sale any that have not been inspected and approved by a Fisheries inspector. Mussels have a distinctive shell that must be familiar to most people ; slate-blue in colour, and shaped

Mussel

rather like the kernel of a very large Brazil nut. They are found in clusters on inshore rocks, jetties, mooring hawsers, and the iron girders of piers. They attach themselves by means of a number of very tough silk-like threads, and quite a lot of force is required to remove them from their roosting place. Many are gathered for use as bait, especially by the Scottish long-line fishermen.

Inside the mussel one sometimes comes across a gristly lump, which many people fear to be some sort of parasitic growth. Actually this is only the mussel's store of spare silken 'anchor ropes', and is quite harmless ; although, of course, it should not be eaten.

Frequently in the gardens of longshore cottages, and sometimes in places quite a long way from the sea, one happens upon large quantities of limpet shells. More than once I have heard people, obviously a little puzzled, discussing these finds. The truth is that at one time limpets were a very

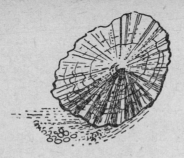

Limpet

popular item of food, and these inland limpet shells are all that is left of some long-departed longshoreman's supper. Similar hoards of shells are found among the remains of primitive man all over the world, from those of the African bushman to the kitchen middens of our own prehistoric ancestors. Just why the limpet should have lost favour is difficult to say, as the young ones, when boiled or fried, are very tasty.

No list of edible shellfish would be complete without some mention of the oyster, although very rarely indeed may they be gathered by the ordinary longshoreman. For the most part they are cultivated in specially prepared beds around the south-east coast, notably at Whitstable, in Kent, Brightling-

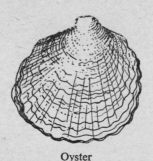

Oyster

sea, in Essex, and in the Thames estuary. Many of these beds, being below the tide line, belong by right to the Crown.

The number of places suitable for oyster culture is limited by several factors, the chief ones being the water temperature, which must not be too cold during the summer breeding season, and the nature of the sea bed. Oysters do not thrive in sandy localities, as grains of sand enter the shell and prevent it from opening and closing properly.

There was a time when British oysters were plentiful, but shortly after the First World War their numbers were decimated by an unknown disease. Unfortunately, the hordes of slipper-limpets and oyster-drills, which prey upon the oyster, were unaffected by the disease, so that even after the epidemic had spent itself the survivors never really had a fair chance to re-establish themselves.

Oysters are bivalve molluscs, allied to the cockle and mussel. As in the case of these other shellfish, they are liable to become polluted when living in impure water, and although unaffected themselves, they can act as carriers for typhoid bacteria, so often fatal to man. For this reason cultivated oysters are subject to Government inspection and other precautions. The produce of the Brightlingsea beds, for instance, spend their last days there in baths of warm, purified sea water, in which they cleanse themselves before being despatched to market.

COCKLES

Before being cooked, cockles should be very thoroughly washed in several waters to remove all traces of sand, and the shells scrubbed. Afterwards they should be placed for two hours in salty water so that they may also cleanse themselves internally.

Roasted
The simplest and most popular method of cooking cockles is to roast them on a tin laid on top of a hot stove. They should be eaten hot with bread and butter.

Boiled, with Prawns
Cockles may also be cooked by dropping them into a pan containing about half an inch of boiling water. Place the lid on the pan, and keep the water boiling briskly until the shells open. Prepared in this way, the cockles are particularly tasty if chopped up, mixed with prawns, and used as a filling for toast sandwiches, with a pinch of pepper and salt to taste.

OTTER CLAMS, GAPER CLAMS, AND RAZOR CLAMS

Boiled
Cook by the method described above for cockles.

Baked
24 clams.
5 medium-sized mushrooms.
3 slices of bacon, previously fried and chopped up.
Salt and pepper ; breadcrumbs ; butter.

Wash the shellfish thoroughly by the method recommended for cockles. Spread them on a tin in a previously heated oven ; then remove from oven when the shells start to open, closing oven door again immediately. Remove the clam meat from the shells and chop it up. Moisten the meat with the clam liquor, and mix it with chopped-up mushrooms, bacon, salt, pepper and sufficient breadcrumbs to bind the other ingredients. Replace the mixture in the empty clam shells and sprinkle with more breadcrumbs ; then add a smear of butter to the top of the mixture in each shell. Finally, replace in the oven, and cook until the covering of breadcrumbs has turned to a golden brown.

Clam Chowder

2 lb. of clam meat—removing meat from shells by the method described in the previous recipe.
4 new potatoes (medium size).
3 onions.
4 oz. fat pork.
¼ teaspoonful of pepper.
2 teaspoonfuls of salt.
1 pint of scalded milk.

Chop up the clam meat, pork and vegetables, but do not mix. Fry the pieces of pork until crisp, and then use the fat to fry the onions, removing them from the pan before they turn very brown. Sprinkle pepper and salt over the clam meat, and place in a saucepan with the pork and vegetables. Pour in enough boiling water to cover ; boil for 20 minutes, and add the pint of boiling milk just before serving.

Clams cooked in Pressure Cooker

After the clams have been thoroughly washed, place them in a pressure cooker with sufficient water for 7 minutes' boiling. Cook at 10 lb. pressure, and after 7 minutes cool off cooker under a running tap. Serve the clams in their shells with melted butter and lemon juice to taste.

WHELKS

These shellfish should be thoroughly washed, and then left in a bath of water for several hours so that they may cleanse themselves internally. Medium-sized whelks make the best eating; the larger ones usually proving to be somewhat tough.

Boiled

The most economical way to boil whelks is in a pressure cooker. They should be given half an hour at 15 lb. pressure. In an ordinary saucepan they need to be boiled in salty water for between 70 and 80 minutes, according to size.

Fried

Whelks may be removed from their shells after being parboiled, then dredged in flour, dipped in beaten egg and breadcrumbs, and fried. They should be served hot with pepper, salt and vinegar.

WINKLES

These ubiquitous shellfish taste not unlike whelks, but being considerably smaller they require proportionately less time to cook. After being thoroughly washed they should be placed in a saucepan, stirred with the hand to make them return into their shells, and then quickly covered with boiling water. A handful of salt should then be added, and the water kept boiling for about 20 minutes.

Removing the meat from the shell requires some skill, and a stout pin. After opening up the disc of horny material that forms the winkle's 'front door', the pin is inserted slantwise into the meat, so that with a slight twist it is possible to 'unscrew' the winkle, as it were, from its spiral shell.

MUSSELS

Baked
2 to 3 dozen mussels, according to size.
2 medium-sized shallots.
2 medium-sized mushrooms.
1 teaspoonful of chopped parsley.
Mixed herbs.

Wash the mussels thoroughly in several waters, then open them by placing them, without water, in a pan over a hot stove. Remove them from the pan as they open and divide the shells, placing two mussels into each half-shell. Sprinkle with a mixture of chopped-up shallot, mushroom and parsley, together with a pinch of pepper and mixed herbs. Over this sprinkle a layer of breadcrumbs and a little olive oil. Place the shells on a baking tin and cook in a moderate oven for a quarter of an hour. Serve hot.

LIMPETS

Boiled and Fried
Wash the shellfish thoroughly in several waters. Place them in a saucepan and boil in salty water for 20 minutes, by which time the limpets will have dropped from their shells. Take hold of the tiny horned head of each shellfish between finger and thumb and remove it with a gentle twist and a pull. If carried out properly this will also remove the limpet's entrails, which look rather like a short length of bicycle valve rubber, followed by a thin, thread-like tube. Remove the tough 'foot' of each limpet and discard. Now chop up the remaining limpet meat and fry until nicely browned, then serve on hot buttered toast with pepper, salt and vinegar to taste.

NOTE: As there are some people who prefer to eat their shellfish raw, it might be as well to mention here that limpets have the reputation for being poisonous when uncooked.

This I am inclined to doubt, but have so far lacked both the courage and the desire to put the matter to the test.

OYSTERS

There are plenty of people who insist upon eating their oysters raw, preferably with a glass of stout. There are also just as many who simply could not face up to such a meal. For the benefit of the latter, here are two recipes for oysters which may appeal.

Fried Oysters

Prepare a batter with $\frac{1}{4}$ pint of milk, $\frac{1}{4}$ lb. of flour, 1 egg, and 1 oz. of melted butter; afterwards adding a pinch of salt and allowing the mixture to stand for about two hours. When this has been done, heat up a pan of cooking fat, and in the meantime gently warm the oysters in a separate pan until a frill begins to form around the edges. Strain off the liquor and, when the oysters have cooled, dip them one by one in the batter and fry them in the fat until golden brown.

Oyster Omelette

Beat up two eggs, then mix with three fried and minced oysters; add the cream off the top of a pint of milk, and a trace of pepper and salt. Beat the mixture again with a fork, then pour it slowly into an omelette pan in which a little margarine or butter has previously been thoroughly heated. Cook and serve like an ordinary omelette.

SHELLFISH GENERALLY

There are some people for whom the idea of eating 'sea-snails' has no appeal, and no amount of coaxing will persuade them to give this form of sea-food a trial. Others, whilst finding them very tasty, cannot digest them. Yet again, some people are quite capable of tucking into a plateful of cockles, say, with no ill effects; whilst clams may thoroughly disagree with them. Because of this, I would recommend anybody eating any kind of shellfish for the first time to do so in moderation.

Those who wish to overcome any repugnance they may feel at the thought of eating 'sea-snails' will probably prefer to chop up the meat after it has been cooked, and use it, with pepper, salt and vinegar, as a filling for sandwiches. In this way they will develop a taste for it without seeing what they are eating. So far as most people are concerned, once they have tasted shellfish their prejudices will quickly disappear.

STRANGE CREATURES OF THE TIDE LINE 5

Already in this book we have discussed some of the edible creatures to be found among the rock pools—the lobsters, crabs, prawns and shellfish. While hunting for the pot, however, the rock-pool fisher will notice many other inhabitants of the inter-tidal waters; some of them strangely beautiful; some grotesque, and quite a number so remarkable in appearance that it is difficult to believe that such things could really exist on this planet.

Even the familiar limpet has some quite surprising habits. When the tide is out it clings firmly to the surface of a rock by means of a muscular sucker, and quite often this suction is so great and so constant that the rim of the shell wears away an oval-shaped groove in the rock. This groove is regarded by the limpet as its home.

At one time it was believed that limpets never left home. However, by marking their shells with different-coloured paints, and by keeping a regular watch on them for days and nights on end, it was eventually discovered that during the hours of darkness, and at high tide, limpets make quite long journeys. In the course of their wanderings these shellfish graze upon the bright green sea-lettuce, plucking off mouthfuls of the weed with a long spiny tongue that is barbed with thousands of tiny, glass-like hooks. A strange feature of these foraging expeditions is that every limpet has a tendency to circle round to the left, so that although it wanders far from its habitual roosting place on the rock, it invariably finds its way back home again at the turn of the tide. Various attempts have been made to deflect limpets from their normal routes, or to confuse their sense of direction by turning them round so that they face in the opposite direction, but always they prove themselves capable of overcoming these ruses. Only when its 'home groove' is destroyed with a hammer and chisel does a limpet begin to look lost and unhappy.

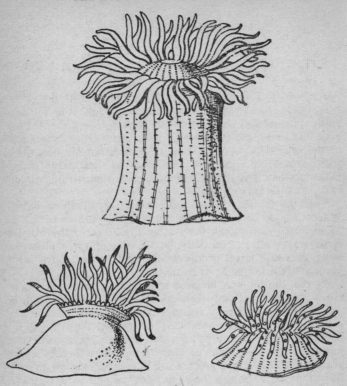

Three types of sea anemone

Peer into any rock pool and you will see that beautiful and fascinating creature, the sea anemone. True, at low tide it may not look particularly interesting, for then it often appears to be a mere rubbery blob, attached to the lower side of a rock. As soon as the incoming tide begins to fill the pool again, however, a strange transformation takes place. The rubbery lump bursts open like a flower bud, and exotic red, brown, green, yellow or multi-coloured 'petals' begin to unfold, waving about gently in the water.

In fact, the sea anemone looks so very much like a flower that it is difficult to think of it as a member of the animal kingdom. Yet science has proved without a trace of doubt that it is. It has no roots, but feeds on small sea creatures, such as prawns or tiny fish, which it paralyses by means of stinging cells concealed in its sensitive tentacles. The helpless victim is then conveyed to the anemone's mouth, and to see the living morsel of food disappear makes it easier to think of the anemone as an animal—and a ruthless one, too.

Its breeding habits, on the other hand, leave one with feelings of mingled amazement and confusion. The anemone will lay eggs; yet at the same time it is quite capable of giving birth to living young by the hundred. Even more remarkable is the fact that cuttings can be taken from certain species as an artificial means of reproduction. Indeed, there would seem to be no end to the surprises which these amazing creatures are capable of springing upon the naturalist. Cut off an anemone's head and it will immediately set about growing another one. Sometimes a single anemone will even turn itself into twins by the simple process of splitting itself down the middle!

It is not surprising, therefore, that such a resourceful creature should live to a ripe old age. The life histories of several aquarium specimens have been recorded, but the most interesting must surely be that of a young anemone which had its origins in a rock pool near North Berwick. In 1828 it was transferred to an aquarium, and during the first twenty years in its new home gave birth to no less than 334 baby anemones, all lusty youngsters. After this praiseworthy effort it rested on its laurels for several years; only to produce, without warning, another 230 offspring in one night. All told, this particular anemone lived for 66 years in the aquarium, and during that time gave birth to over 700 living young.

Incidentally, those people who own a sea-water aquarium will notice a peculiar thing when they introduce an anemone into the tank. For a long while afterwards the creature will fold and unfold itself at regular intervals, corresponding to the rise and fall of the tides in the rock pool that was its original home. Why this should happen in a tank of static water, perhaps many miles distant from the tidal sea, must remain a matter for conjecture.

There are other marine creatures which possess habits as mysterious as the rhythmic opening and closing of the captive anemone. For instance, certain crabs take on a darker hue as the tide ebbs, and then turn lighter again with the flood. Like the anemone, these crabs keep up this habit long after they have been taken from their native rock pools and placed in an aquarium tank. Moreover, despite various attempts on the part of their human captors to confuse their time-sense, the crabs will maintain the rhythm of their colour changes with extraordinary accuracy.

Scientists, carrying out experiments upon some of these crabs, kept them in an aquarium tank that was lit continuously with electric lights. The fact that the creatures thus had no means of telling night from day did not upset them in the least, and they continued to darken regularly at an hour corresponding exactly with the time of low tide in the rock pool from which they had been taken. They even kept pace with minor daily changes in the times of the tides—changes so complicated that the scientists themselves had to make continual reference to Admiralty tide tables!

Later on, crabs were taken from different parts of the coast, where the times of the tides varied by several hours. Although they were kept alongside each other, none of the crabs was confused by the colour changes of its companions, and over a period of several weeks each kept to the time of ebb tide on its own particular stretch of coast.

There have been numerous other examples to show that crabs are both adaptable to circumstances and rugged individualists. Consider, for instance, the story of a half-grown edible crab that was caught in a lobster pot, and despatched to a fishmonger's shop at Tipton, in Staffordshire. On arrival it eluded the boiling pot, and began to make itself useful by catching the mice which infested the shop. The amazed fishmonger, realising that here was one crab that was worth more to him alive than dead, provided it with a bowl of salt water. In between spells of bathing in the bowl, the crab continued its hunting activities, and at the end of the first week in its new home had acquired a reputation as a mouser that any cat might have envied. Its activities were even reported in the national daily papers.

While 'winkling' among the rocks it is not at all unusual to come upon a shell containing what many people suppose

Hermit crab

to be a baby lobster. This is, in fact, the so-called hermit crab, which uses a discarded winkle or whelk shell as a temporary lodging. In this way the crab protects its tender and vulnerable tail, which is conveniently shaped to fit snugly into the corkscrew spiral of the shell.

After a brief and adventurous free-swimming infancy, the young hermit crab usually chooses a winkle shell as its first rock-pool home. But as it grows older, and increases in size, it finds it necessary to move into a larger whelk-shell

The hermit crab changing its shell

residence from time to time. Eventually, after perhaps ten years, it will be occupying the largest whelk shell it can lay its claws on.

Hermit crabs are, in fact, always on the look-out for a bigger and better home, and a lot of fun can be had by putting one or two into a bowl of sea water, and providing them with a selection of winkle and whelk shells to 'try on for size'. They seem to have great difficulty in coming to a final decision, and the more shells you provide them with the greater will be their dilemma!

A hermit crab carrying an anemone

Quite often the shells occupied by the larger hermit crabs are weighed down by all sorts of passengers cadging a free ride, such as barnacles, parasite worms, and a very beautiful species of sea anemone known as *Adamsia palliata*. Naturalists often quote this partnership of the hermit crab and the anemone as a classic example of commensalism—a scientific word which is used to describe a state of affairs in which two different types of creature live together for their mutual benefit. Should anything threaten to attack the hermit crab it withdraws into its shell, leaving the anemone to fight off the intruder with its stinging tentacles. In return, the crab carries the anemone round on its back, sharing the food it catches with its jockey-cum-bodyguard.

That there is a genuine understanding between hermit crab and anemone is made obvious whenever a crab decides to move into a larger shell. After crawling out of its old shell, the crab detaches the anemone and sets it up on top of the new home. The anemone plainly approves of this treatment, because it is by nature almost as much of a 'sticker' as the limpet, and without its co-operation the little hermit would never be able to dismount it from the old shell. A mutual understanding such as this would be remarkable anywhere in the realm of nature, but when one of the creatures is such a humble form of life that it is little more than a vegetable the situation defies human comprehension. Scientists are still puzzling over this problem.

Many sorts of crab are great experts in the art of camouflage, and they go to great lengths to conceal their true identity. The spider crab, which often finds its way into the baited drop net of the prawning enthusiast, will nip off cuttings of seaweed and sponges, and stick them on its spiky shell. The cuttings grow and multiply, and the crab is transformed before long into a wandering marine garden.

Another strange inhabitant of the sea which finds its way to rocky stretches of our coasts is the octopus. Although the British species is no man-eater, the sudden clutch of its sucker-studded tentacles has made many a rock-pool wader utter a yell of fright; whilst its appetite for lobsters and crabs has made an even greater number of fishermen utter a fine selection of hearty curses.

The octopus is said by scientists to possess a very high level of intelligence, and observations have shown that it will even build itself a house. This it does by piling small boulders on top of one another to form a sort of dry-stone walling—if such a thing as a dry-stone wall is possible in a world of water. The octopus leaves an opening in one wall to act as a doorway, often screening it with bunches of seaweed. Inside this door it will lie in wait, ready to stretch out a tentacle and grab some unfortunate crab or lobster when the opportunity presents itself. With the aid of its other tentacles, and a horny, parrot-like beak, the monster will then tear its victim limb from limb, and devour it piecemeal.

In view of this, one would scarcely expect the female octopus to be a fond mother. Yet, after she has laid her eggs, she will attend to them for weeks on end as devotedly as a broody hen. The octopus, in fact, is full of surprises. When in a hurry it moves by jet propulsion, swimming backwards at a terrific speed with its siphon pipe squirting water, and its eight tentacles streaming out behind its body. When pursued by an enemy, such as a conger eel, it will also lay a 'smoke-screen' by ejecting a cloud of sepia, and in this way often contrives to make good its escape. It is also able to change the colour of its body to match its surroundings; a

An octopus

characteristic which helps to make it a star turn in any large salt-water aquarium.

A starfish stranded on the seashore does not look particularly interesting, but, as is so often the case with marine life, its appearance is very deceiving. There are actually several different kinds of starfishes, but the type most people are familiar with is flat and stiff, and possesses five arms, or rays. 'Slow but sure' might well be this starfish's motto, for even when it is in a tearing hurry it takes nearly twenty minutes to travel a single yard. No wonder it sometimes gets left high and dry when the tide goes out!

Turn a starfish over on its back and you will notice that on the under-surface there are hundreds of tiny protuberances, arranged in pairs. These are its feet, each one being a hollow tube operated by a system of hydraulic ducts, and having a suction disc at the tip. Near the extremity of each arm there is also a single, unpaired protuberance containing one of the starfish's 'eyes'. When an eye is being used the tip of the arm on which it is situated is raised slightly to increase its efficiency. Also on the underside of a starfish's body is its mouth, although it is too small to admit many of the mussels, limpets, crabs and oysters which form the main part of its diet. However, the starfish is able to overcome this difficulty quite simply. It merely thrusts its stomach out through its mouth, and digests its food before swallowing it!

You may well wonder how a sluggish creature like the starfish can possibly open the shell of a mussel or oyster in order to get at the meat inside. If you have tried to do this

Starfish opening a cockle

yourself you will know that it is no easy task, even when using the blade of a strong knife to give added leverage. The answer lies in the suckers at the tips of the starfish's hundreds of tube feet. It attaches these to either side of the shellfish and just pulls—and pulls.

To drag a limpet off a rock requires a direct force of thirty pounds or more; yet, incredible though it may seem, the flabby-looking starfish is capable of doing just that. It straddles the limpet's tent-shaped shell; places the ends of its five arms firmly against the rock and, using the suction discs on the inner parts of its arms, enfolds the limpet's shell in anything but a fond embrace. A prolonged tug-o'-war ensues, and the limpet, becoming weary, eventually relinquishes its grip on the rock.

The starfish, however, does not have things all its own way. Like most creatures of the sea it has plenty of enemies. A dog whelk may settle on its back and suck out its entrails.

51

Or a large fish may seize one of its arms as a preliminary to gulping it down whole. In this latter sort of emergency the starfish will often shed its captured arm and creep away unnoticed by the fish. This method of escape is not quite so drastic as it sounds, for in due course another limb will grow to take the place of the one that has been lost. This in itself is remarkable enough. But what is really amazing is that a discarded arm of a starfish is actually capable of growing another body, and four more arms!

Another strange creature found around the coasts of Britain is the sea urchin. More or less spherical in shape, it

A sea urchin

is covered with a veritable forest of waving spines, tube-feet and microscopic pincers. These appendages, which are often brightly coloured and numbered in their thousands, are used by the urchin for a variety of purposes: feeling its way, walking, keeping itself clean, catching and gathering its animal and vegetable food, and passing these morsels to its mouth.

Incidentally, the sea urchin's mouth is worthy of close inspection. It incorporates five sets of grinding teeth, known collectively as Aristotle's lantern. Around the mouth there radiate five grooves, which divide the outside of the urchin into segments, like the 'quarters' of an orange. These grooves give a clue to the origin of the sea urchin, which is, in fact, little more than a starfish that has had its five arms folded over backwards until they meet.

The interior of this 'rolled-up starfish' is reinforced by a limy, pentagonal shell, and these sea urchin skeletons, like tiny, brittle gourds, are to be seen occasionally on gravel beaches, washed up by the tide. As a rule they find their way into the oddments bag of the longshoreman beachcomber, for they are pretty things, and there is always a demand for them as mantelpiece ornaments. Study one of these shells closely and you will notice that it is composed of hundreds of separate interlocking pieces, like a jig-saw puzzle. This arrangement enables the sea urchin to expand its shell as it grows—fresh deposits of lime being continually

Shell of a sea urchin

added to the edges of each piece of the 'jig-saw' during the creature's lifetime.

As a point of interest, there is a British member of the sea urchin tribe, *Echinus esculentus*, that is extremely good to eat. The Romans knew all about it, and considered it to be a great delicacy. When boiled it has a taste very similar to crab, although quite often it is eaten raw. The coral-coloured spawn, which is found inside the urchin during the spring months, is also much in demand by a minority of people who know a good thing when they taste it.

A more distant relative of the starfish is the sea cucumber, which is usually to be found firmly squeezed into some rockpool crevice. The commonest type is comparatively small, and is known very appropriately as the sea gherkin. When taken out of the water it shrivels up into a most uninteresting, slug-like object, but left to its own devices in the rock pool it is quite beautiful, with a satiny-white skin, a waving array of tentacles, and a curious, vegetable-like bunch of gill-plumes sprouting from the end of its headless body.

If you are lucky you may also come across the big brother of the sea gherkin, commonly known as the cotton spinner. It derives this name from its peculiar method of defending itself against attack. When threatened by a fish or lobster it will eject from its stern a sticky white substance, not unlike raw cotton in appearance, which fouls the enemy's gills, often causing death from suffocation. Meanwhile, the cotton spinner, looking a little thinner, but otherwise unconcerned, crawls away to take refuge in the nearest crevice among the rocks.

Along boulder-strewn shores a teeming multitude of queer creatures live a cramped existence beneath every flat stone, and it will repay you to turn over some of the smaller rocks and take a look underneath. Shore crabs, ragworm and baby butterfish will scuttle, squirm and wriggle out of reach, leaving behind the less nimble creatures for your leisured inspection. On the underside of a projecting lip of rock you may happen upon the beautiful sea lemon. As its name implies, this member of the slug family is yellow, and does, in fact, bear a remarkable resemblance to a lemon that has been cut in half from end to end. At the front of this luscious-looking creature a pair of small horns stick up perkily, whilst the stern is decorated by a feathery tuft. This latter appendage, however, is not a tail which the sea lemon wags when it is feeling pleased with life. It is a very delicate and important piece of apparatus, the gills through which this 'living fruit' breathes.

Beneath another boulder you may come across something which lacks the beauty of the sea lemon. Most people, in fact, would call it downright revolting. It is a black worm, incredibly long, and thin, and twisted, so that it looks rather like a tangled mass of bootlace liquorice that has reposed for many weeks in a schoolboy's pocket. Charles Kingsley, in his book, *Glaucus*, gives us the following graphic—one might almost say horrific—account of this worm's appearance and habits:

'. . . . in turning this stone, we must pay a fine for having done so ; for there lies an animal, as foul and monstrous to the eye as "hydra, gorgon, or chimera dire", and yet so wondrously fitted for its work, that we must needs endure for our own instruction to handle and look at it. Its name I know not (though it lurks here under every stone), and should be glad to know. It seems some very "low" Ascarid or Planarian worm. You see it? That black, slimy, knotted lump among the gravel, small enough to be taken up in a dessertspoon. Look now, as it is raised and its coils drawn out. Three feet! Six—nine at least, with a capability of seemingly endless expansion ; a slimy tape of caoutchouc, some eighth of an inch in diameter, a dark chocolate black, with paler longitudinal lines. Is it alive? It hangs helpless and motionless, a mere velvet string across the hand. Ask the neighbouring Annelids and the fry of the rock fishes, or put it into a vase at home, and see. It lies motionless, trailing itself among the gravel ; you cannot tell where it begins or ends ; it may be a strip of dead seaweed, *Himanthalia lorea,* perhaps, or *Chorda filum* ; or even tarred string. So thinks the little fish who plays over it, till he touches at last what is too surely a head. In an instant a bell-shaped sucker mouth has fastened to its side. In another instant, from one lip, a concave double proboscis, just like a tapir's, has clasped him like a finger, and now begins the struggle ; but in vain. He is being played, with such a fishing-rod as the skill of a Wilson or a Stoddart never could invent ; a living line, with elasticity beyond that of the most delicate fly-rod, which follows every lunge, shortening and lengthening, slipping and twining round every piece of gravel and stem of seaweed, with a tiring drag such as no Highland wrist or step could ever bring to bear on salmon or trout. The victim is tired now ; and slowly, yet dexterously, his blind assailant is feeling and shifting along his side, till he reaches one end of him ; and then the black lips expand, and slowly and surely the curved finger begins packing him end foremost down into the gullet, where he sinks, inch by inch, till the swelling which marks his place is lost among the coils, and he is probably macerated into a pulp long before he has reached the opposite extremity of his cave of doom. Once safe down, the black murderer contracts again into a knotted heap, and lies like a boa with a stag inside him, motionless and blest.'

On this rather awe-inspiring note let us leave the rock pools and walk along the shore to a different sort of hunting-ground. On our way, though, it will pay us to keep an eye on

The egg case of a dogfish

the high-tide line, where strange objects are often to be found, washed ashore from regions some distance out to sea. For instance, amongst the stranded seaweed one frequently finds a mermaid's purse. However, it is no use looking inside for coins of Neptune's kingdom, nor even for a string of cowrie shells, because the maidens of Atlantis are not really so care-less as all that. These brown pouches, with a horny 'tail' at each corner, are the egg cases of the dogfish and skate—those of the dogfish being oblong, and those of the skate being more or less square.

Amongst the rubbish of the tide line the beach hoppers are always very active, scavenging everything that is in any way edible, and generally tidying the place up. Here and there we see numbers of these frisky little crustaceans leap-frogging over the pebbles, advancing before the incoming tide. But it is when we pick up a large bunch of tangled seaweed that we really see them *en masse*. There are so many of them that their myriads of tiny legs make a sort of whispering sound as they move frantically in search of fresh cover. Within a matter of seconds there is not a beach hopper to be seen ; they have all gone to ground amongst the shingle, or found a new hiding-place under another bunch of seaweed. Beach hoppers have a good reason for not liking to make themselves conspicuous, for there are several types of sea bird which regard them as very tasty morsels.

After trudging along the shingle for some time we arrive at a spot where, at low tide, an expanse of salt water becomes trapped by a ridge of pea gravel to form a sort of long, narrow lagoon. In this sheltered stretch of water there flourishes the eel-grass, or *Zostera marina*, which is really a freshwater rush that has run away to sea. Wade into this submarine meadow, thrusting your hand net under the over-arching, emerald green leaves, and before long you will have caught enough prawns and shrimps for your tea.

Down near the roots of the grass you will capture the peculiar-looking mantis prawn, which has a body like a miniature lobster, and a pair of spiky forearms with which it adopts an attitude of religious devotion, like its tropical, landlubberly namesake, the praying mantis. When boiled and shelled, its body is extremely good to eat. But be careful when picking it out of the net. Those spiky 'hands' can give you a nasty jab.

Also to be found occasionally on the bed of this lagoon is the pistol-packing prawn. There is no need to be alarmed, though ; it is not really so dangerous as its name would have you believe. A bright, angry pink, it is so called because when caught it will snap one of its claws at you, making a noise which, if amplified, would indeed sound like a six-shooter in the hands of a trigger-happy cowboy.

Thrusting our net among some tufts of green ribbon weed, we begin to catch numbers of tiny chameleon prawns. It is well worth while keeping a few alive and putting them in a bowl of sea water, first of all with some red seaweed, and then, a few days later, with some pieces of green sea-lettuce. You will then see how these little creatures manage to change their colour scheme to blend with their background. During the hours of darkness, however, no matter what the colour of their surroundings may be, they change to a beautiful shade of blue.

The fairy shrimp also adapts itself to its surroundings, although the method is different. Its body is transparent, like that of H. G. Wells's 'Invisible Man', so that when it swims past a bunch of seaweed you do not see the shrimp, but only the seaweed on the far side of it.

The most extraordinary inhabitant of the eel-grass lagoon to find its way into your net, however, will surely be the so-called Caprella, or ghost-shrimp. Although very small and quite useless as food, it is well worth while taking a few home to add a humorous touch to your aquarium, if you have one. For, with its whiskery face, beady eyes, gesticulating 'arms', long, skinny waist, and legs all clustered at the tail end of its body, it has a ridiculously human appearance. Normally it crawls along the stems of seaweed by alternately arching and extending its body, but at frequent intervals it pauses and stands upright, teetering precariously and waving its arms frantically, like a very inexpert tight-rope walker. Quite often two of these comical crustaceans will meet face to face while walking in opposite directions along the same weed stem. The dumb show which follows puts one in mind of an early silent Charlie Chaplin film. Neither of the animated skeletons will give way to the other, and they stand there gesticulating as though they were engaged in a terrific verbal battle. Eventually, with ironic bows, they solemnly turn their backs on each other, and pick their way gingerly back along the weed stem towards the place from whence they originally came. On this return journey they may meet other shrimps going the other way; in which case the same, ridiculous clowning act will probably take place all over again!

Have you ever come across a slug that flies? You will discover just such a creature grazing on the leaves of the eel-grass, and to make matters more complicated it is referred to by most people as the sea hare. With a stretch of the imagination the broad tentacles on its head do make it look rather like a tiny, prick-eared hare; although, because the creature also has a smaller, secondary pair of horns, I think our local Dorset name for it—the sea cow—is a better description.

All told, the sea hare is an odd sort of an animal. It carries a shell on its back, yet hides it under a layer of skin. On either side of the shell this skin forms two large lobes which the slug is able to use as a pair of wings, so that sometimes it goes flying clumsily through its watery element, like the proverbial cow jumping over the moon. When fearful that some fish is going to make a meal of it, the sea hare will also throw out a deep purple 'smoke-screen', which effectively confuses its pursuer, and enables the hard-pressed mollusc to make good its escape into the depths of the eel-grass jungle.

One does not need to probe the mysteries of the weedy lagoon for long before the hand net brings to light a most peculiar little tube-shaped fish. As you pick it up in your fingers it gazes at you out of its beady little eyes, as though trying to think up some excuse for its unusual appearance. And no wonder—for this little fellow has a snout so long and thin that it looks like the nozzle of a fireman's hose!

This is the pipe-fish, a relative of the quaint little sea horse which is common in the Mediterranean and parts of the Atlantic, but which only occasionally drifts into British waters. Like its foreign cousin, the pipe-fish is a poor swimmer, and spends most of its time hanging on to a stem of eel-grass or seaweed, looking puzzled and rather helpless.

As we have already learnt, the creatures of the sea are full of surprises, and our new-found friend is no exception. For instance, it is the male pipe-fish who acts as 'mother' to the young ones. In early summer, when the female lays her eggs, her mate sticks them on to his abdomen, and then—if he be one of the larger species—protects them with two flaps of very thin skin. This gives him the appearance of wearing a plastic apron, and makes him look very domesticated and married. When eventually the eggs hatch out he releases his offspring by performing a complicated series of physical jerks. But even after they have gained their freedom the babies, when frightened, still cling by their tails to their father's apron strings.

On flat sandy beaches it is no unusual thing in summer to see hundreds of jellyfish stranded by a combination of tide and onshore wind. Lying there, motionless and flabby, they are rather repulsive-looking objects, and it seems impossible that they could ever appear otherwise. But go out in a rowing boat on a sunny day when the sea is calm and clear, and you will see jellyfish drifting along just beneath the surface, as colourful and beautiful as flowers.

The jellyfish—a very primitive, one-celled animal—was one of the earliest inhabitants of the sea. Even as far back in time as five hundred million years ago it was well established, and probably looked very much like many of the species which roam the seas today. Those jellyfish seen most frequently around British shores belong to the family known as *Medusæ*. They have a body shaped like an open parachute and, although largely at the mercy of the ocean currents, are able to swim feebly by a motion which resembles the repeated opening and closing of an umbrella.

Along some stretches of beach there are occasions when the numbers of jellyfish amount to what is almost a plague. Swimming in the sea becomes extremely unpleasant, not only because one is repelled by the feel of their clammy caresses, but also because there are always plenty of people near at hand to warn you that jellyfish can sting—and sting badly.

As a matter of fact, though, only a few of the many different types of jellyfish found around our coasts are likely to cause serious inconvenience to a swimmer. One of these may be recognised by the brown and white markings which radiate like spokes from its centre; whilst trailing from the outside of its body are the two dozen stinging tentacles which ensure its unpopularity. Two other species which should also be given a wide berth are the large blue *Cyanea lamercki,* and the yellow-tinted *C. capillata,* both of which possess eight tentacles capable of setting up a most painful irritation.

What purpose do these venomous tentacles serve, apart from stinging bathers? Well, a clue to the answer lies in the fact that the jellyfish is closely related to the sea anemone. The tentacles grasp and paralyse small fish, conveying them to the jellyfish's mouth, which is situated in the centre of the underside of its body.

Fortunately, however, the jellyfish found most often around British shores is quite harmless to human beings. It is the pretty *Aurelia aurita*, which has four violet loops visible through its almost transparent body. These loops are, in fact, the creature's reproductive organs, and as the 'love life' of *Aurelia aurita* is fairly typical of most other species of jellyfish we will give it some attention.

There are both male and female jellyfish, but they breed more like plants than members of the animal kingdom. The males release their sperm into the sea, and it is in this way that the females, swimming nearby, become fertilised. The *Aurelia aurita* is a more devoted mother than most jellyfish, retaining her tiny eggs in a special 'inside pocket' until they hatch. The larvae, which do not resemble their parents at all, drift around for a while, and then attach themselves to a rock on the sea bed.

After a while the infant jellyfish begins to take on the appearance of a tiny sea anemone, with four rudimentary tentacles grouped about a central depression that is actually an ever-open mouth. The tentacles grow longer, and repeatedly increase in number until, finally, the jellyfish-child is the proud possessor of thirty-two writhing feelers. At this stage side shoots are thrown out, and the creature seems almost to settle down to a vegetable-like existence.

Day by day, month by month, the seasons of the sea come and go. After several years the wearying observer might be excused for thinking that by some error of Nature the jelly-fish eggs had turned themselves into a macabre, carnivorous underwater plant—and that there the matter was destined to end. But then a strange thing happens. This peculiar marine growth begins to cast off dozens of tiny trans-

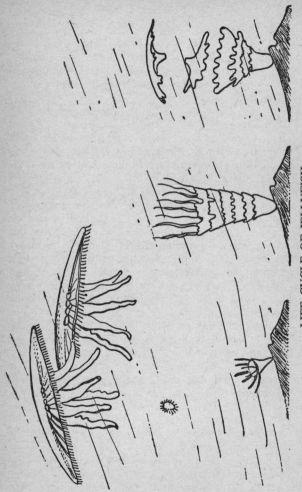

LIFE CYCLE OF JELLYFISH

Stages in the growth of *Aurelia aurita* from the point where the larvae is dropped by the mother and attaches itself to a rock, to the stage when it eventually begins to cast off dozens of tiny transparent discs which in turn become jellyfish

62

parent discs, none of them larger than the head of a tin-tack. By the rhythmical opening and closing motion of these discs, however, one is able to recognise them for the finished article—freely swimming jellyfish, complete with a fringe of microscopic tentacles.

Off the coasts of Devon, Cornwall and south-west Ireland one very occasionally sees a different sort of jellyfish, mainly blue in colour, which floats on top of the water like a blown-up plastic bag. This is the Portuguese Man-o'-War, and the swimmer would be wise to steer well clear of it, because its stinging tentacles are not only extremely venomous, but often trail through the water for a distance of twenty feet from the bladder-like body. I was once stung by one while swimming off the South African coast, and for days afterwards my chest and back were marked with long 'whip-lash' weals, along which, at about half-inch intervals, itching, watery sores appeared. Even so, after comparing my symptoms with others who had suffered the same misfortune, it seemed as though this particular jellyfish must have let me off lightly.

Philip Henry Gosse, in his book, *A Year at the Shore,* published in 1865, quoted the following report from a certain Mr. Bennett who, in the cause of science, deliberately allowed himself to be stung by a Portuguese Man-o'-War:

'. . . on seizing it by the bladder portion,' writes Mr. Bennett, 'it raised the long cables by muscular contraction of the bands situated at the base of the feelers and, en-twining the slender appendages about my hand and finger, inflicted severe and peculiarly pungent pain, adhering most tenaciously at the same time, so as to be extremely diffi-cult of removal. The stinging continued during the whole time that the minutest portion of the tentacula remained adherent to the skin. I soon found that the effects were not merely confined to the acute pungency inflicted, but produced a great degree of constitutional irritation: the pain extended upwards along the arm, increasing not only in extent but in severity, apparently acting along the course of the absorbents, and could only be compared to a severe rheumatic attack; the pulse was accelerated, and a feverish state of the whole system was produced; the muscles of the chest even were affected, the same distressing pain felt on taking a full respiration as obtains in a case of acute rheumatism. The secondary effects were very severe, continuing for nearly three-quarters of an hour; the duration of the pain being probably longer, in

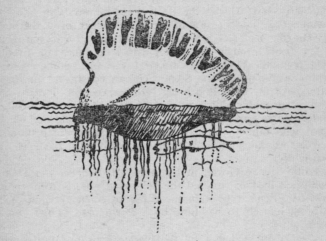

Portuguese man-o'-war

consequence of the time and delay occasioned by removing the exciting and virulent tentacula from the skin, as they adhered to it, by the aid of the stinging capsules, with an annoying degree of tenacity. On the whole being removed, the pain began gradually to abate; but during the day a peculiar numbness was felt, accompanied also by an increased temperature in the limb upon which the stings had been inflicted. For some hours afterwards the skin displayed white elevations or weals on the parts stung, similar to those usually seen resulting from the poison of the stinging nettle. . . . To remove the irritation, at first cold water was applied, but this, instead of alleviating, increased the evil: an application of vinegar relieved the unpleasant symptoms, and olive oil has produced similar beneficial effect. I have observed that this irritative power is retained for some weeks after the death of the animal in the vesicles of the cables; and even linen cloth which had been used for wiping off the adhering tentacles, when touched, still retained the pungency, although it had lost the power of producing such violent constitutional irritation.'

The above gruesome details remind us once again that the sea is full of 'monsters', both big and little, and that the eternal struggle for existence of its inhabitants is a grim and deadly business. Even the heavily armed jellyfish has its enemies in the tiny, sea-going violet snails, which cruise along over the ocean wastes, nibbling at the jellyfish's body whenever they feel hungry.

Yet even the violet snail is at the mercy of wind and current, and countless thousands of them are stranded every year on the beaches of Britain. In certain places along the western seaboard of Ireland the longshore naturalist will come upon small sandy coves that are almost covered with their pretty, delicately tinted shells.

Eventually, however, the ebbing tide that has uncovered so many interesting things for our inspection will begin to turn. As the waves begin clawing their way up the shore again we must, for the time being, bring our wanderings at the sea's edge to an end. But we can console ourselves with the thought that there will be another low tide tomorrow, producing just as many new and unexpected discoveries to fascinate us. The strange creatures which inhabit the waters around our coasts are almost limitless in their numbers and variety, so that even a whole lifetime spent down by the shore would scarcely be sufficient to explore all the wonders to be found there.

To most people seaweed is singularly uninteresting stuff;
slimy to the touch, smelly when stranded on the beach and
decomposing, and affording a treacherous footing when one
is scrambling over the longshore rocks at low tide. Although
there are hundreds of different sorts of seaweed, the majority
of people are only familiar with about half a dozen varieties,
and it is doubtful whether many could actually put a name
to one of them with any degree of certainty. Yet seaweed
can be beautiful—and interesting—as those people know who
have gone out in a small boat when the water is clear, and
gazed down into a marine garden. In their natural element
these plants of the tidal waters have a grandeur that remains quite unsuspected by anyone who has only seen the
dead specimens which are washed ashore after every storm.

The seaweed zones around the world's land masses are
of the greatest importance, as they are the ultimate source
of life for all marine animals. They provide food for many
types of fish and molluscs when living, and for countless
more lowly creatures, such as worms and small crustaceans,
when dead and decomposing. These small vegetarian animals
are themselves the food of those slightly larger inhabitants of
the shallow offshore waters, which are in turn eaten by other
predatory fish. Thus the chain of life progresses outwards and
downwards into the mid-ocean deeps; where, because there
is continual darkness, plant life is non-existent, and all the
inhabitants are carnivorous.

The largest types of seaweed are generally to be found
in the deeper coastal waters, for there they remain comparatively undisturbed by waves and tides. Seaweed growing
close to the shore is usually fairly small, with pliable fronds
or threads which are able to adapt themselves to rough water.
Inshore weeds, owing to the fact that they get more sun-
light, are also lighter in colour as a rule, ranging from reds

and browns to varying shades of yellow and green. Red laver and Irish moss are two of the best-known red sea-weeds to be found is British waters; the familiar bladder wrack belongs to the intermediate brown group, whilst the green laver, or sea-lettuce of the rock pools, is perhaps the most common type of green weed.

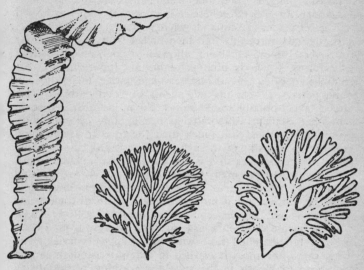

Seaweed   (i)   Purple laver
             (ii)   Round polyides
            (iii)   Interrupted stenogramme

Many seaweeds are quite high in nutritional value, and are widely used as food in those over-populated parts of the world where land crops alone are insufficient to feed the people. They are eaten as vegetables and savouries, and are also used in the form of soups and jellies. In Japan the scientific cropping of seaweeds has for a long time been an important industry, and the Americans, with their natural gift in such matters, have invented a name for this marine farming. They call it aquiculture.

Apart from the Japanese, many other nations have been using seaweed as food for hundreds of years, including Chinese, Malays, Polynesians, Norwegians and, nearer home, the Irish and Scottish crofters. The purple laver, which grows on exposed low water rocks along many parts of the British coast, has a considerable sugar content. It possesses a pleasant 'sharp' taste, and is sometimes eaten on toast as a savoury. In Ireland, where it is known as 'sloukawn', and to a lesser extent in Scotland, where it is referred to as 'sloke', it is washed thoroughly and then boiled with a little vinegar for several hours. On being allowed to cool, an olive-green jelly forms, which is both palatable and nourishing. Apart from being eaten spread on bread-and-butter, this jelly is in some parts used for making a sort of fried oatmeal cake. Green laver, usually found rather closer inshore, is used in somewhat similar fashion. It has broad, shiny green fronds.

Another seaweed still much used for food in Ireland and Scotland, although not in such quantities as during the lean times of the last century, is the carragheene, or Irish moss. It is a short, tough, many-branched weed, often to be found growing as a thick carpet on flat rocks near the lower tidal limits. It varies in colour according to the district, being sometimes red, purple, chocolate-brown or yellow. Those who gather the weed on a large scale often do so from a boat, using a long-handled rake with thin, slightly curved teeth. Afterwards, the moss is washed in sea water and spread on the shore to bleach in the sun; the washing process being repeated several times at intervals of a day or so. When this has been done the weed is boiled in milk to form an extremely pleasant and satisfying blanc-mange. There is also a large demand for Irish moss from the commercial manufacturers of table jellies and other gelatinous products.

Another red seaweed closely resembles Irish moss, and is known to scientists as *Gigartina stellata*. During the last war this weed suddenly acquired considerable importance as a source of agar-agar, a substance much in demand by bacteriologists as a medium for the cultivation of germs for scientific study. Before the war Japan was this country's only source of agar-agar, and when supplies suddenly ceased in

1939 the whole of our intricate system of bacteriological research and diagnosis was jeopardised at a time when it was most urgently needed. Today, supplies of Japanese agar-agar are available again, but most of that used in Britain is still being produced from 'home-grown' seaweed.

Many marine plants are also of considerable value to longshore farmers, and all over the British Isles, from the

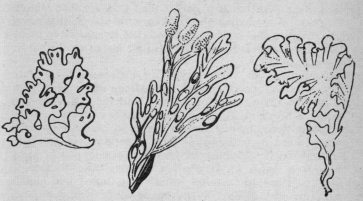

Seaweed (i)   Irish moss
        (ii) Twin bladder wrack
        (iii) Broad ulva

market gardens at Marazion, in Cornwall, to the crofts in the Orkneys and Shetlands, thousands of tons of seaweed are gathered after every storm for use as manure. In many instances the right to collect seaweed is an important part of a tenant-farmer's lease. It has been said that, in terms of present-day artificial fertilisers, a single ton of dry drift- or tangle-weed is worth rather more than £6. Moreover, the seaweeds add humus to the soil, a thing which artificial fertilisers fail to do. Although not so rich in phosphorus and nitrogen as farmyard manure, seaweed is extremely rich in potash, and is excellent for root crops such as potatoes and mangolds, and for cabbages, lettuces, brussels sprouts and broccoli. It is important, though, that seaweed should be spread on the land as soon as it is collected, as it quickly loses its fertilising properties when left standing in heaps.

Certain types of seaweed are also useful as stockfeed, and it is not unusual to see cattle of longshore farms browsing upon patches of marine plants exposed at low tide. Indeed, on one of the islands of the Orkney group there are sheep which exist largely on seaweed, and it is said that, when killed, their flesh is much darker than that of other mutton as a result of the iodine absorbed from their somewhat novel diet. They are also reputed to be practically immune to many ovine diseases, a fact which is also attributed to their high 'iodine content'.

The burning of various types of drift-weed to produce kelp—a source of soda, potash and iodine—was once a major industry in many parts of Ireland, and the highlands and islands of Scotland. This longshore trade has almost vanished of recent years, mainly due to the discovery of more economical sources of supply for these important raw materials. The seaweed is still collected, however ; but instead of being burnt it is baled by hay-baling machines and shipped in coasting vessels to factories, where it is turned into alginic acid. This acid, or its salts, has many commercial uses: it is used in the leather trade, in the manufacture of certain plastics, fireproofing and waterproofing compounds, cosmetics, jams, jellies, glues, and any number of other products in everyday use.

Despite all these demands for seaweed, vast quantities go to waste all round our coasts. People living on the coast who possess an enquiring turn of mind might do worse than to familiarise themselves with the various types of seaweed in their district, and to find out some of the uses to which they can be put. Experimenting with recipes could be interesting, and—who knows?—there is always the possibility that the knowledge gained may one day prove to be really useful!

Most visitors to the seaside derive considerable pleasure and amusement from watching the habits and antics of the sea birds. The gulls, of course, attract most attention: they are noisy, cheeky, gregarious and, like lots of human beings, they seem to enjoy squabbling amongst themselves.

The most argumentative member of the gull family is undoubtedly the Greater Blackbacked Gull, a hefty bird that will not hesitate to rob another gull of some tit-bit that happens to take its fancy. It also has a bloodthirsty habit of devouring the eggs and young of other sea birds, and has even been known to kill new-born lambs. Towards its own offspring, however, it is extremely devoted, and to illustrate this fact there is the story of a parent Blackbacked Gull that swooped down upon a naturalist who was examining one of its fledgelings. With its claws the large bird snatched the youngster from the surprised man's clutches; then flew away with it towards the sea, and there dropped it gently on to the surface of the water. Soon the other parent also appeared, and when last seen the three birds were swimming hard along the coast, presumably bound for some place where they could continue the business of raising a family safe from the attentions of meddling Man.

As its name implies, the Greater Blackbacked Gull's mantle and wings are sooty-black; whilst the rest of its plumage is white. When approached on the ground it will often adopt an arrogant stance, and in the company of other gulls it is usually the last to take to the wing. It is an ugly-looking bird when seen at close quarters; there is a hawk-like shape to its eyes which seems to give it a perpetual scowl, and on the lower mandible of its yellow beak there is a crimson patch which at first sight looks like an adhering piece of raw meat. Also, it is not nearly so sociable as most of the other longshore gulls, and does not nest in large colonies. In

May or June it chooses a suitable place on top of a high cliff and there builds a rough and ready sort of a nest, making use of such materials as seaweed, sticks, grass, or even scraps of old fishing nets and pieces of rope. The two or three eggs are usually buff or olive, with dark brown spots, and the young birds, when they are fledged, are mottled buff and brown, so that they bear little resemblance to their parents.

Greater blackbacked gull

This drab-coloured juvenile plumage is, in fact, a common feature among the various types of gull which nest around the British Isles, and it is usually three, four, or even five years before these young birds finally acquire their 'grown-up' dress. In practically every case the change is a gradual one, taking place over several moults. A period of adolescence lasting for perhaps five years may sound a long time for a bird, but it must be remembered that gulls—especially the larger species—live to a ripe old age. It is, of course, impossible to estimate with any certainty the average life-span of a gull, because there is no Registrar for Births and Deaths in the sea-bird world; but a gull that was kept in captivity is recorded as having lived for forty-one years.

The Lesser Blackbacked Gull is fairly common around the

British coasts before it sets out on its winter migrations, but many people fail to recognise it because its name is rather misleading. It is a medium-sized gull, and its back is not really black, but a sort of dark slate-grey. The only black to be seen in its plumage is at the wing-tips. Quite often it is mistaken for the Herring Gull, which is of identical size and

Blackheaded gull

has very similar markings. The back of the Herring Gull, however, is of a lighter hue, and the legs and feet are pink, whereas those of the Lesser Blackbacked Gull are bright yellow.

A much more graceful-looking bird than those mentioned so far is the Blackheaded Gull. It is very common on inland waters as well as by the sea, but many people fail to recognise it because of its misleading name. Its head is not black but chocolate-brown, and then only during the breeding season. In winter the only markings on its head are a dark brown streak near the eye. During both winter and summer the upper parts of this bird are a bluish-grey, and the underparts pure white. Legs, feet and beak are a deep, rich red, and the wings are slender, making it very agile when in flight. Normally, the Blackheaded Gull feeds on fish, worms and longshore grubs, but at certain times of the year it is a common sight to see large flocks of them turning and twisting high up in the air as they pursue swarms of flying ants and other insects. Londoners will be familiar with their aerobatics, for these gulls are numbered among those which swoop around the Thames bridges, catching in mid-air the scraps of food thrown to them by passers-by.

Summer visitors to the English coast will discover that there is yet another sea bird that belies its name, the so-

Kittiwake

called Common Gull. From April to late August it is most uncommon. This is because at that time of the year it is busily engaged at its breeding haunts, which are to be found mainly around the northern coasts of Scotland and Ireland. The most favoured nesting sites are small islands in the middle of sea-lochs, and boggy moorlands overlooking the sea. During the autumn and winter months, however, the Common Gull may be seen in large numbers all round the coasts of England and Wales, often in the company of other gulls. In appearance it is rather like a small and less preda-tory-looking Herring Gull. The beak, legs and feet are yellowish-green, and these are helpful distinguishing features when the bird is seen at close quarters.

Another dainty-looking gull is the Kittiwake, but it is not often seen around the English coasts as it spends most of its life far out to sea. In size and colour the adult bird is not unlike the Common Gull, but the legs and feet are almost black. It is a most graceful bird when on the wing, and as it skims and hovers over the crests of the waves it will utter its name with a shrill, far-crying 'Kitti-wa-a-ake.'

In early spring it begins to feel the urge to breed, and large colonies gather on precipitous cliff ledges along various parts of the coast, ranging from Land's End and the Scillies to the Orkneys and Shetlands. Two or three off-white eggs, with brown and grey spots, are laid in May and June, and by August the young birds are trying out their wings. The plumage of these juveniles is most distinctive, with black streaks over and behind the eyes, a broad black collar on the back of the neck, and a black band across the tip of the tail. When the wings are outspread in flight there is also a well-defined V-shaped black band along the leading edge of the upper surface of the wings. All told, the Kittiwake is a delightful bird to watch, and a walk along a cliff path overlooking one of their nesting colonies can be extremely interesting.

Along open beaches all round the British coast there will often be seen groups of smallish birds with long, slender wings and very distinctive forked tails. These are terns, or 'sea-swallows' as they are sometimes called, and they are most likely to attract one's attention when they are feeding on shoals of small fish, such as whitebait. Quite often this happens within fifty feet or so of the shore, each bird hovering and wheeling above the shoal for a few seconds before suddenly diving down to pick up one of the tiny silvery fish in its beak. Along the south coast of England the seine-net fishermen watch the activities of the terns with great interest, for by betraying the presence of whitebait shoals they often indicate the whereabouts of mackerel, which also feed on these small fry. The tern is, in fact, often referred to by fishermen as the 'mackerel bird.'

Several species of tern may be seen around the coast, but the majority of them are comparatively rare, and the type most likely to be seen is the Common Tern. It has a tapering, orange-red bill tipped with black, and a patch of black on the head which extends down the nape of its neck. Its back is a very pale grey, its underparts white, and legs and feet red. It is essentially a summer visitor, arriving with the first shoals of surface feeding fish round about the middle of April. In May, groups of terns congregate in large, close-packed colonies known as 'terneries', each female laying her two or three eggs on the ground, often without bothering to build a nest. By late June and early July the young terns begin to hatch out, and when only three days old they start exploring the world about them for the first time. One of the

Common tern

best-known terneries in the south of England is situated on the Chesil Beach, in Dorset, close to the famous Abbots-bury Swannery.

Another bird whose home is normally the open sea, but which visits the British coast to breed, is the Great Skua. There is something hawk-like about this powerful bird, with its fierce eyes, thick-set, dusky-brown body, and curved, predatory beak. Moreover, it is as ruthless as it looks, for it obtains much of its food by harrying terns and gulls until, in fright, they disgorge the fish which they have recently eaten. The skua then pounces on these 'secondhand' meals and gulps them down with obvious relish.

During the breeding season, when a good proportion of its time is spent on land, the skua will also kill and eat small birds and insects, and rob other birds of their eggs and nest-lings. Yet, cruel though it may be, it is no coward, and will defend the territory around its own nest with pluck and tenacity, making repeated 'dive-bombing' attacks on any intruder. On the ground, when angry or excited, it also makes a great to-do, calling with a harsh shriek, whilst at the same time spreading out its wings behind its back and advancing belligerently with outstretched neck.

The Great Skua is not seen around our coasts very often as it breeds among the islands north of Scotland, after which most of the birds fly away into the Atlantic. A few, however, travel down the east coast, and these may be seen by the late holidaymaker in September and October.

There is another skua with similar habits, but of different

Great skua

appearance, which also breeds among the northern isles. Known as the Arctic Skua, its body is considerably smaller and more streamlined than that of the Great Skua, and as a rule it is a uniform sooty-brown; although a minority of birds possess whitish underparts. The tail is wedge-shaped, and the two central feathers are about three inches longer than the others. The Long-tailed Skua is somewhat similar in appearance, except that its two central tail feathers may protrude for as much as eight or nine inches. It does not visit Britain to breed, but is sometimes seen in autumn as a passage migrant along the east coast.

Occasionally, at certain times of the year, the person standing on the seashore will have his attention attracted by a medium-sized sea bird which skims just over the tops of the waves, banking steeply first to one side and then to the other. Its back and the upper surface of its slender, rakish-looking wings are black, while underneath it is white, so that every time it banks in flight the bird appears suddenly to change colour. This is the Manx Shearwater, a relative of the Storm Petrel and the Albatross, and normally its home is the open sea. In early spring, however, the shearwaters begin making their way towards various breeding islands off

Manx shearwater

the west and north coasts of Britain and Ireland, where the females lay their single white egg at the end of a burrow, which the birds dig for themselves. Among the most popular and accessible groups of islands used by the shearwater are the Scillies, Skokholm and Skomer off the Pembrokeshire coast, and Bardsey, which lies to the north of Cardigan Bay.

Anyone who enjoys camping in unusual places would find a night spent near one of these shearwater colonies an unforgettable experience. A mere daytime visit, on the other hand, would prove disappointing, for even in May and June, at the peak of the nesting season, not a single shear-water is to be seen during the hours of daylight. This is because one member of each pair of birds is away all day quartering the sea for fish, while its mate sits patiently in the darkness of the nesting burrow, brooding over the single precious egg. As dusk approaches, however, shearwaters begin to appear over the horizon in ones and twos. Converging on the island, they gather into great restless groups of flashing black and white wings, as they wait for the onset of darkness. Only when the last faint orange tint of the afterglow has faded from the western sky do these birds of the open ocean summon up sufficient courage to venture over the land. Out of the night come weird strangled cries as they call out to their mates, and from the depths of the nesting burrows come muffled responses, which frequently sink to an eerie whimpering moan. The incoming birds, unused to alighting on anything but the face of the sea, make ungainly crash landings amongst the heather and bracken; each waddling away afterwards to its own particular burrow. The sitting bird, on being relieved, shuffles out of the hole, and after conversing noisily with its mate for a while, flounders away in search of a good taking-off point. It has to do this because on level ground its legs are too short to allow its wings sufficient scope for it to become airborne. Thus, at all shearwater colonies there are certain rock outcrops which are used by the birds as 'spring-boards', and the person who hides himself near one of these places will see— if he possesses good night vision—a strange procession of shuffling shapes making their way to the edge of the rock. One after another the birds spread their wings and step out into the night sky, to be glimpsed for a brief moment against the starlit sea as a swiftly moving silhouette, before finally disappearing into the darkness.

Storm Petrels, known to sailors as Mother Carey's Chickens, are often found nesting close to shearwater colonies. No larger than swallows, they are brownish-black, except for a white base to the tail, and anyone who has made a long ocean voyage must have been impressed by the sight of these tiny birds fluttering erratically like moths over the waves, many hundreds of miles from the nearest land. They look such fragile creatures, and the ocean is so vast and unruly.

Yet the Storm Petrel makes the Atlantic its home right through the winter months, and during stormy periods it often sleeps for only a few seconds at a time, floating on the water in the troughs between the great waves. Almost by instinct, it would seem, the petrel rises into the gale again just in time to avoid each foam-capped crest as it bears down on it with a roar. Sometimes these winter gales continue for weeks on end, and it is not surprising that sailors the world over regard this tiny sea bird with admiration,

Storm petrel

and never cease to wonder at its ability to survive in a world in which every elemental force seems bent on its destruction. In fact, on a number of occasions during the last world war the crews of torpedoed vessels, adrift in their lifeboats, were saved from utter despair by catching a glimpse of one of these birds. It seemed to the storm-tossed seamen that if such fragile creatures could battle against the might of the ocean and survive, then surely they could too!

Storm Petrels are by nature nocturnal creatures, and in the days of sail seamen used to regard their appearance on the wing in broad daylight as an omen of bad weather. Possibly there was a good deal of truth in this belief, for these birds deliberately fly in search of storms. Strangely enough, they do this because they are comparatively weak upon the wing—the explanation being that in rough seas they are able to obtain shelter from the strong ocean winds by flying in the troughs between the waves. At such times they

80

often skim to and fro only a few inches above the surface, sometimes actually helping themselves along by dabbing at the water with their tiny webbed feet. In rough seas they also find food more plentiful, for their diet consists of plankton, and these microscopic forms of sea life are brought to the surface in turbulent water. The churning propellers of a steamship have the same effect of stirring up the plankton, and it is for this reason that at night Storm Petrels can sometimes be seen following the phosphorescent wake of a vessel.

Only in spring, when they feel the mating urge, do these lonely little birds head for land. Among the Scilly Isles, and on Lundy, they begin to arrive round about the end of April, but breeding islands farther north are not occupied until a few weeks later. The single egg is white with a few brown spots, and this is sometimes deposited at the end of a burrow, although more often the nesting place is a natural crevice among the boulders, or a hole in an old stone dyke. Like the shearwaters, Storm Petrels only visit and leave the colony after nightfall, serenading each other as they do so with strange whimpering cries, which sound very queer indeed when heard coming from the ground beneath one's feet on a dark night.

The Fulmar is also a member of the petrel tribe, although to the casual observer it would seem to bear a closer resemblance to a Herring Gull, for it is a greyish-winged bird of about the same size. When in flight, though, it can be distinguished from a gull by its wings, which are long and narrow, and are not angled at the shoulders when gliding. When seen at close quarters the bird's greenish beak is almost certain to catch the attention, for on top of it the nostrils are enclosed in a pair of horny tubes—a common feature among the petrels.

To ornithologists the Fulmar is something of an enigma, for in recent years it has undergone a remarkable increase in numbers. Until 1878 the only British nesting place of this bird was St. Kilda, a remote island that lies a hundred miles west of the Scottish mainland. For centuries the islanders had kept the Fulmar population at a fairly level figure by killing a proportion of the young birds for food. Every breeding season thousands of squabs were taken from their nests, plucked, and salted down for winter use. Then, quite suddenly, and for no apparent reason, the Fulmar population on St. Kilda began to increase, until eventually overcrowding compelled a group of birds to colonise Foula, in the Shetlands. This marked the beginning of a rapid spread of the Fulmar, so that today the bird may be seen nesting in

Fulmar

great numbers all round the coast of Scotland, and also in smaller and newly started colonies around the west coast of Ireland, and parts of England as far south as Devon and Cornwall. Many scientists have tried to discover the reason for this sudden increase in the Fulmar population. One likely explanation is that the advent of power trawling provided the birds with an increased supply of fish offal food.

One of the largest sea birds to be seen around the coasts of Britain is the Gannet, which has a wing span of over six feet. It is easily recognised by its white plumage, dark brown wing-tips, long, buff-tinted neck and head, and large spear-shaped beak. When on the wing its flight is most distinctive, consisting of several easy, purposeful wing beats, followed by a long, steady glide.

The Gannet, or Solan Goose as it is often called, feeds entirely on living fish, which it catches in a most spectacular manner by diving headlong into the water from a height of fifty to eighty feet. The bird drops into the sea at a great speed with its wings folded—a feat which is accompanied by a considerable splash. To the onlooker, in fact, it would seem as though the bird's audacity must result in injury, but the force of its impact against the water is cushioned by a layer of special air cells beneath the skin of the breast. When under the surface the bird partly opens its wings again, using them for steering[1] purposes in much the same way as the hydroplanes on a submarine. The fish, when caught, is swallowed under water, and within a second or two the bird comes to the surface again and flies away.

Gannet

Gannets may be seen fishing off most parts of the coast at some time during the year, although they are, of course, most common in the neighbourhood of their breeding islands. Bass Rock and Ailsa Craig are two notable Scottish Gannet colonies; whilst on Grassholme, off the Pembroke-shire coast, there are some 6,000 nesting pairs belonging to the Royal Society for the Protection of Birds. Gannets are also frequently seen off the west coast of Ireland, and the

---

1. The word 'steering' is used here in a three-dimensional sense.

writer knows a fisherman of County Kerry who suffered ship-wreck through one of these birds. Out mackerel spinning in his canvas curragh, he had just caught a fish and thrown it into the bottom of his frail craft when the silvery gleam of its scales caught the eye of a passing Gannet. Before the fisherman had realised what was happening, the bird had wheeled and dived right through the bottom of his boat—taking the mackerel with it!

The breeding season of the Gannet starts early in April, when quite often a hundred or more pairs of birds may be seen building their grass and seaweed nest on one not very large ledge of rock. The single egg is bluish-green in colour, overlaid with a chalk-white deposit, and this is incubated by the bird placing its large webbed feet around it, and then sitting on its feet. This unusual method would appear to be rather inefficient, because the bird has to sit like this for over six weeks before the egg hatches. Another three months passes after that before the young Gannet leaves its nest, during which time the rock ledge becomes covered with an extremely odiferous layer of decomposing fish. When the young bird has reached the fledgeling stage it is black speckled with white on top, and whitish-brown underneath. Not until after three or four years, and a long succession of moults, will it acquire the almost white plumage of an adult bird.

When the young Gannets finally leave their parents they seem compelled by a strong instinct to turn their backs on the breeding colony and swim straight out to sea. No one has yet discovered why this should be ; nor do we know how far the young birds travel like this before taking to the air. Recoveries made from ringed birds, however, tell us that these young Gannets eventually migrate to north-west Africa for the winter, while the majority of older birds find a living from November to February among the shoals of fish in the Bay of Biscay, and off the coast of Portugal.

Quite often, when walking along a rugged stretch of coastline, one sees a large, long-necked, black-plumaged bird standing on top of a rock, its beak raised towards the sky and displaying a white patch under the chin. Frequently, too, its wings will be open and spread out to dry in the wind and sun. This is the Common Cormorant. With its jet black 'coat', white 'collar', and extended 'arms', it looks very much like a clergyman addressing his flock, and for this reason the bird is often referred to in the south of England as the Isle of Wight Parson.

Common cormorant

The Common Cormorant lives entirely on fish, which it catches by swimming under water. It possesses an extremely voracious appetite, and is particularly fond of small flat fish —two facts which ensure its unpopularity among fishermen. During the breeding season it may desert the coast for a while and build its nest on the shores of some inland water, or even in a tree. Its three or four eggs have a greenish shell, but this colour is hidden by a chalky outer deposit. The young birds, when fully fledged, have a creamy breast deepening to brown around the edges.

A close relative of the Common Cormorant is the somewhat smaller Shag, a uniformly black bird with a greenish sheen to its plumage. During the breeding season it wears a curly black crest, which gives it a tousle-headed appearance, as though it had just been 'pulled through a hedge backwards'. Unlike the Common Cormorant, its diet consists

Common guillemot

mainly of coarse fish of little commercial value. It distrusts inland breeding sites, and will almost always be found nesting close to the sea, on cliff ledges, or in small caves.

Several other sea birds swim under the water for their food, and one which is seen quite frequently around our coasts is the Common Guillemot. It is easily recognisable in summer by its sooty-brown head, neck, back and wings; white underparts, and long, tapering beak. When the bird is swimming on the surface of the water its white underparts form a sort of 'Plimsoll line', and it is not until the bird takes to the wing that its snowy breast becomes very obvious. In winter a patch of white also appears on its throat and cheeks.

Strangely enough, the Common Guillemot is able to swim much faster under the water than on the surface, propelling itself with its wings and steering with its webbed feet. During the winter months it does not voluntarily frequent land, although during rough weather many get driven ashore. Also, in recent years, large numbers have suffered a lingering death through coming into contact with patches of oil sludge discarded by shipping. With their feathers clogged they are unable to fly, and usually finish up by being washed ashore in a weak and helpless condition. A few lucky ones are picked up by bird-lovers and have their feathers cleaned with repeated applications of lard before being released again at the water's edge. The vast majority, however, either starve to death, or fall victim to the shore rats. Should you ever decide to play the Good Samaritan to an oil-clogged sea bird, do not on any account attempt to clean its feathers with petrol. True, this would remove the oil-sludge, but at the same time it would destroy the natural waterproofing properties of the bird's plumage. In some species this would cause the sea bird to drown as soon as it was re-introduced to its natural element.

During the breeding season, which extends from about the middle of May until July, the Common Guillemot is a fascinating creature to watch. Its legs are placed very far back on its body, so that on land it has to adopt an upright stance, and this characteristic, coupled with its 'black suit and white shirt front', gives it an almost human appearance at times. It builds no nest, but lays its one enormous, pear-shaped egg on a flat-topped stack of rock, or cliff ledge.

Guillemots are very sociable birds, and in some places they nest so closely together that the eggs get kicked around like footballs by alighting birds, so that their fond owners are for ever waddling around in their efforts to retrieve them. In fact, the activities of a large guillemot colony resemble more than anything else a game of musical chairs played by a gathering of rheumaticky gentlemen in evening dress. The eggs are very varied in colour, ranging from creamy white to delicate shades of greens, blues, and pinks, scribbled over with black and brown markings.

An excellent place to watch the nesting antics of Common Guillemots is at Flamborough Head, on the Yorkshire coast. Here, too, the holidaymaker can see the eggs being gathered by iron-nerved men, known as 'climmers', who allow themselves to be lowered over the cliff-edge on the end of a rope. The eggs are rich in albumen, and are used mainly to clarify wine, and in the dressing of patent leather. The sale of curiously marked eggs to naturalists also forms a profitable side-line.

Considering the risks involved, the price charged for the eggs is very reasonable. To prove this point the men of Flamborough Head are in the habit of relating an adventure which once befell a climmer called Sam Leng. Having filled his bag with eggs, Sam gave the signal to his mates on the cliff-top to haul him up again. A moment later he felt the rope begin to vibrate as they pulled on it, but to his surprise he did not move. His immediate reaction was to glance up to see what the trouble might be, and it was then that he got a nasty shock. In one place the apparently strong rope had stretched, strand by strand, until it was no thicker than a man's finger. Sam waited with clenched teeth for the rope to break, but by some miracle it never did, and after what seemed like an eternity he found himself being dragged over the cliff-edge by the outstretched arms of his comrades. From that day on, Sam Leng knew what it was like to have one's life 'hanging by a thread'.

Another bird that nests on the rock ledges under Flamborough Head is the Razorbill. It is, in fact, very similar to the Common Guillemot, both in its habits and general appearance. The most obvious distinguishing feature is its large black beak, which is deep and flattened at the sides, with a vertical white mark near the middle. In summer there is also a narrow white streak across the face from the beak to the eye, but in winter this almost disappears. In its place, however, there appears a patch of white on throat and cheeks.

Although the Razorbill may pride itself on the size of its beak, there is another bird which has an even larger one. This is the Puffin, and so extraordinary is the appearance of this tubby little fellow that one might almost call him the clown of the sea-bird world. His upperparts and the collar round his neck are black; his cheeks, face and underparts are white, and his triangular beak is bluish-grey at the base, red at the tip, and has red and yellow stripes in the middle.

To enhance this 'glorious technicolor' effect, his legs and feet alternate between bright orange in summer and yellow in winter.

As a rule Puffins are only seen by landsmen during the breeding season, when these birds abandon their maritime existence along rocky stretches of the western and northern coasts. In May or June a single white egg is laid in a rock crevice or rabbit burrow, and six weeks later the young

Puffin

Puffin is hatched. To the exotically-hued parents the fledge-ling, with its short black beak and black feet, must prove something of a disappointment, but this does not prevent them from plying their offspring with plenty of affection and fishy tit-bits. Mother and father Puffin both go a-fishing to satisfy junior's appetite, and each will catch as many as ten small fry, one after another, arranging them neatly in their huge beaks. How they manage to catch the last few fish without losing those they have already caught is a mystery which naturalists are still trying to solve.

When busy feeding their young, Puffins pay little atten-tion to a human onlooker, and it is fascinating to sit near a burrow and watch the constant comings and goings of its temporary occupants. Swooping in to land, the Puffin's splayed-out, orange feet are used for steering and braking in place of its almost absent tail. This is followed by a quick, waddling dive into the mouth of the burrow, and the next we see of our friend is a flamboyant beak and a mischievous eye peering out at us again a few seconds later. Sometimes a sudden inadvertent movement on our part may startle him, and out of his burrow he will scuttle, hurrying so fast that his little legs are quite unable to keep up with him, and he falls over on to the end of his beak. The slope down from the mouth of the burrow to the cliff-edge does the rest, and over and over he rolls in a series of somersaults. At the cliff-edge he spreads his wings and flies away over the sea, treating us to a final backward glance of mild surprise, as though wondering how so many bewildering things could have happened to him in such a short space of time!

Thousands of years ago, when Man was first learning how to make things, someone discovered that it was possible to cross a river by sitting astride a tree-trunk, using the hands as paddles. From this idea there developed two of the very earliest types of boat, the dug-out canoe and the raft. Both are still used by primitive peoples in various parts of the world, but in this country our ancestors slowly improved their boats, stage by stage.

After dug-out canoes had been in use for many hundreds of years the Ancient Britons began building coracles. These were small one-man boats made by covering a circular framework of bent hazel sticks with the skins of animals. Coracles are still used by fishermen on several rivers in Wales, and this is especially interesting because the Welsh are directly descended from the Celtic Britons of old, who first invented this type of boat. It would seem more than likely, therefore, that in Wales the art of making coracles has been handed down from father to son without a break since prehistoric times. In fact, the only way in which the present-day coracle differs to any marked degree from that used by the Ancient Britons is that the wooden framework is covered with tarred canvas, instead of the skins of animals.

A little later on an improved sea-going type of coracle was developed. It was built from the same materials as the river coracle, but was shaped like a large canoe, and was rowed with oars. Examples of these have also survived, and hundreds are in everyday use on the west coast of Ireland, where they are known as curraghs. They are versatile craft, and sometimes carry a small lugsail when there is a favourable wind. Sheep are ferried to and from the islands in them, and once, off the Kerry coast, I even saw a trussed-up heifer being rowed across the Sound to Great Blasket Island.

Built with a pronounced sheer, the early forms of curragh

Coracle, as used by the Ancient Britons

proved themselves to be extremely buoyant and seaworthy, and old records show that some quite long voyages were made in them. A skin-covered boat had one great disadvantage, though: it was very easily holed when landing on a rocky shore. Therefore, when men began to grow more skilful in the use of tools they started making their boats stronger by covering the framework with planks of wood instead of the skins of animals. Before long they were building boats very similar to the ones we know today.

People from places inland, holidaying by the sea, are often amused by the way in which local fishermen are apt to stop work and gaze for five or ten minutes on end at any strange craft entering the harbour. To the inlander all boats look pretty much alike, and they find it difficult to believe that any small craft could possibly merit such elaborate scrutiny. Yet to the seaman every boat has a character of its own; a

Later version of coracle, known as a 'curragh', seen mostly on the west coast of Ireland

character that is reflected in the shape of its hull and the cut of its sails. Boats play an all-important part in his life, and it is natural for him to study a craft he has not seen before, and judge for himself how it would behave in a seaway.

The inlander during his brief holiday-visits to the sea cannot hope to become as knowledgeable about boats as the professional fisherman ; such wisdom is inbred as well as acquired. But much can be learnt from studying carefully how various types of boat have been built, and pondering over the reasons for these varying methods of construction. For instance, it will be noticed that most of the small open boats have their strakes, or boards, attached to the ribs so that they overlap one another. A boat like this is said to be clinker-built. It is the sturdiest type of wooden boat there is, and is the best sort for dragging up a stony beach.

Larger boats, which are kept in harbours, are usually built with their boards laid side by side, so that the hull presents a smooth surface to the water. Boats of this type are said to be carvel-built. Generally they are not so strong as those which are clinker-built, but they are usually faster.

Until the middle of the last century it was customary for even quite large offshore fishing boats to be undecked, and this caused the loss of hundreds of lives every year. Without the protection of a deck, a boat had only to ship a large beam sea and she was doomed. This state of affairs was brought to the notice of Parliament under unhappy circumstances, when hundreds of fishermen went down with their boats in the terrific gale which struck our coasts on the 19th August, 1848.

The result was a Government enquiry, which led to the fitting of decks to the majority of our larger fishing boats. This was one of the most important advances made in the design of the old sail-powered fishing fleet. Another improvement resulted from the development of trawling by the fishermen of Brixham, in Devon. A vessel with a very considerable sail area was needed in order to drag a heavy beam trawl along the sea bed, and the eighty-foot, ketch-rigged Brixham trawler was evolved to perform this task. These wonderfully fast and seaworthy craft will be remembered for

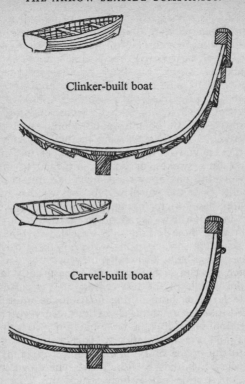

Clinker-built boat

Carvel-built boat

as long as seamen talk about ships. Several used to be entered for important yacht races by their fishermen crews, and on a number of occasions they carried off all the prizes. In one race a Brixham trawler is said to have sailed round the triangular course at an average speed of twelve knots, easily outstripping the streamlined yachts against which she was competing.

The first half of the present century witnessed an almost complete change-over from sail to mechanised power in our fishing fleet, so that today Britain's only link with the sailor-men of the past lies in the amateur yachtsmen who cruise around our coasts in their thousands every summer. Some of these amateur seamen are very skilful indeed, sailing their small craft single-handed, or with a crew of only one or two, across vast stretches of ocean. Many readers will recollect the voyages of the *Nova Espero*, a tiny sailing boat, about twenty feet long, which made the double crossing of the Atlantic a few years ago. Just try to imagine a twenty-foot boat—it is not much longer than a fair-sized rowing skiff on the River Thames!

There can be no denying that the introduction of mechanical power made the lot of the fisherman much easier. The engine not only propelled the boat; it was also coupled to a winch which could be used for hauling in the trawl, nets, or long lines. This saving of labour meant that less men were required in a crew, so that each man's share of the proceeds from the catch was increased proportionately. On the other hand, the capital outlay and general running costs were far greater, and as trawling was carried out more intensively so the fishing grounds nearer home became almost worked out. This in turn made it necessary to build larger deep-sea trawlers which could range far abroad in search of fresh fishing grounds. These big craft were able to use heavier gear, so that even greater havoc was wrought on the new fishing grounds. In this way the cod, hake and flatfish stocks steadily diminished, until before long the trawler skipper was obliged to seek his catch hundreds of miles from port, often in Arctic waters. Needless to say, the expenses of a fishing trip of this nature are colossal.

How these problems will be solved remains to be seen; perhaps science will produce some cheaper form of motive power which will cut down the fisherman's expenses. If so, it is unlikely that there will be any outstanding alterations in hull design. Even the revolutionary conversion from sail to mechanical power did not bring any noticeable change in this respect. Fishermen are very conservative, and rightly so; for the sea itself and all its dangers are also unchanging. Thus, the hull of the modern motor trawler is based upon that of the ketch-rigged Brixham trawler of the last century; and the diesel-powered pilchard boat of the Cornishman possesses lines almost identical to those of the lugger used by his grandfather. It is the same the world over. In the fjords of Norway I have seen open fishing boats which have borne a most striking resemblance to the long-boats of the Vikings of old.

Where the smaller types of pleasure craft are concerned, however, there have been some quite revolutionary changes in recent years. Sailing and outboard-powered dinghies built of marine grade plywood are now to be seen all round our coasts, and many up-to-date yacht designers have produced kits which enable the amateur handyman to build himself a prefabricated plywood boat at a very reasonable cost. Perhaps the most surprising development in recent years, though, is the fibreglass boat. Molten glass is spun into very fine threads and woven into a sort of cloth, which is then moulded into the required shape of the hull. A boat built in this way is both tough and durable, and, of course, the glass hull is impervious to rot and attack by marine worms. We have certainly travelled a long way since our ancestors first began to hack out their canoes from the fallen giants of the primeval forests, thousands of years ago!

Already in this book we have discussed at some length the possibilities of prawning and lobstering from the shore. Although this can be done with considerable pleasure and profit, it will probably not be long—human nature being what it is—before the rock-pool enthusiast will be hankering to try his luck from a boat. He will feel certain that if only he could drop his nets into deeper water he would obtain much better catches.

Such aspirations are founded on sound reasoning as well as wishful thinking, and for the amateur longshoreman who has discovered that he is really keen on prawning, crabbing, lobstering, or fishing, it would be well worth his while to try to obtain the use of a boat. On many parts of the coast it is possible for visiting fishermen to hire boats by the hour, and this should not prove too expensive if several go out together and share the cost.

For the person who lives on or near the coast, however, there is nothing so wholly satisfying as having a boat of one's own. It need not be an expensive proposition; especially if the prospective buyer is willing to bide his time and purchase during the winter months. At such times bargains do occasionally appear in the advertisement columns of local newspapers.

Assuming that the average person seeking a boat knows enough to tell the difference between a sound craft and one that is full of leaks, I propose to confine my advice to those points which may help to prevent unsuspecting buyers from falling foul of the more carefully camouflaged snags.

Don't be misled by appearances. A freshly-painted boat may look very pretty; but it may also be a 'whited sepulchre'. See that none of the ribs are cracked, or the strakes warped away from their rivets. Pay particular attention to the stem, which is usually one of the first parts of a boat to become

D 97

affected by rot. A jab here and there with the pointed blade of a pen-knife will tell you whether the wood is hard and sound, or 'spongy' and rotten.

Boats are frequently offered for sale as being 'in need of a few repairs'. A handyman, on inspecting the boat, will know at once whether or not he is capable of tackling the job. It is the man who is none too skilful with tools who is most likely to over-estimate his ability to make the necessary repairs. Where there is the slightest doubt on this score it is best to have nothing to do with the boat. The price of materials and labour is so high these days that to employ someone else to make the boat seaworthy would probably cost more in the long run than the boat itself was worth. Whenever possible, therefore, buy a boat that is sound, and—better still— already in the water. It should then be possible to take it out on trial to see how it handles. Even if most of your time in it is to be spent anchored over a fishing-ground this last point is still quite important.

One of the main considerations when choosing a boat is to make quite sure that it will be suited to the job it will be called upon to perform, and the conditions it will have to stand up to. For inshore fishing an ordinary small rowing boat, capable of being fitted later on with an outboard motor if required, is all that is really necessary. In place of the motor, however, some will wish for a centreboard and sail.

If you intend going out by yourself on occasions, then an 11 or 12 ft. dinghy will be sufficiently big for your needs. Indeed, if it is to be kept on a steeply shelving beach that is about the largest sort of boat you will be able to launch and haul up unaided. If you live close to a small harbour, and decide to keep it there, this problem will not arise, of course ; although it is still a good idea to keep your boat as small as possible. For one thing, boats need to be painted at frequent intervals, and in this respect a small one saves a lot of time, trouble and expense.

It is not generally realised by those who have had no previous experience in such matters just how tricky launching a small boat on an exposed stretch of beach can be. Before buying a boat that is to be kept on a beach, therefore, it is essential that one should be quite clear upon several points. Firstly, a boat, if it is to stand up to being repeatedly dragged over a pebble beach, must be built of stout timbers, and protected with a liberal coating of paint or tar. Usually a clinker-built craft is favoured for this rough sort of usage.

Flat-bottomed boats are not usually associated with the sea, but the coble used by the professional north-east coast fishermen is an exception that has proved itself through the centuries to be a very seaworthy beach boat. Therefore, do not despise a boat just because it is a 'flattie'. It may prove just the thing for inshore fishing, and if the bottom is built of good stout timber there is no reason why it should not stand up to being hauled over pebbles. There will be no wear on the sides of the boat, so it is of little importance if they are of lighter construction.

There are, however, two features which every boat that is to be launched from a shelving beach must possess. It must have a high, clean-swept prow, and a transom that rises well above the waterline. The reason for this is that where the water deepens very rapidly, as for example on Dorset's Chesil Beach, the waves break very close inshore, and curl over to form a sort of rotating cylinder of water. When being launched from the sloping beach a boat meets these waves whilst at a disadvantage, for the bows are pointing downwards, and should they not possess the correct lines they would tend to lunge their way into the rolling mass of water rather than rise over it. A swamped boat would be the inevitable result.

Similarly, when landing, the stern of the boat has to take the full force of the waves, and with the bow grounded on the beach it is particularly vulnerable. Therefore, not a second should be lost between touching the shore, grabbing the bow-strop, and dragging the boat out of reach of the waves. Carelessness in this operation can easily result in the boat swinging broadside on to the waves, overturning, and being badly damaged—and it can all happen in a few seconds!

On the steeply shelving Chesil Beach, where quite often the waves only break when they are within five or six feet of the shore, many of the older rowing boats are built on the lines of a whaler, with a 'bow' at either end. This certainly lessens the risk of swamping when landing, but the design is going out of fashion as it does not lend itself satisfactorily to the fitting of an outboard motor.

Whilst on the subject of keeping a boat on the beach, it might not be out of place to consider the legal position as regards foreshore rights and the payment of dues. In legal parlance the foreshore is that land which 'lies within the ordinary flux and reflux of the tides'. Normally, it belongs to the Crown, unless it has been proved to be part of a manor, or to have been granted by the Crown at some past date to an individual or public authority. It has been said that when anyone has the right to gather wrack or take royal fish from the foreshore, then that foreshore may be presumed to be part of his manor. The owner of a stretch of private beach, however, is still bound by law to permit adjoining landowners to pass freely to and from the beach to their land, and to fish and beach their boats, provided that such has been the local custom since time immemorial.

When a boat is kept in a harbour—other than a purely natural one—it will, of course, be necessary to pay harbour dues. In the case of a small boat these should not amount to much, possibly only a guinea or two for the season, and on a rocky or otherwise difficult stretch of coast this additional outlay would be money well spent. Nevertheless, keeping a boat in a harbour is not always an advantage. Many small fishing harbours dry out at low tide, and for several hours every day one is unable to enter or leave them. On the other hand, it is usually possible to launch a small boat from a beach at any state of the tide.

It may be thought that keeping a boat in a harbour will save it from the wear and tear it would suffer if dragged repeatedly over a stony beach, but the fact is that pebbles on the seashore are generally smooth and round as the result of the wearing action of the waves. In a crowded fishing harbour, on the other hand, boats are constantly encountering all manner of mishaps. The waters of even the most sheltered harbour are by no means smooth when a gale is blowing from an unusual quarter, and at such times boats jostle one another to the detriment of their paintwork, or rub against rough harbour walls. On a beach, though, the boats would have been dragged well up above the reach of the highest tides, where they could come to no harm.

Admittedly, it is better for a boat to remain in the water all the time rather than have its timbers dried and warped on a sunny beach, but a canvas sheet tied over the hull in hot weather can prevent this from happening.

From the remarks so far contained in this chapter it will be seen that there is really very little to choose between keeping a small boat on the beach or in a harbour. Local conditions must be the deciding factor in every case. Your best plan, therefore, if in doubt on this point, is to approach the local longshore fishermen for their advice. It will be given readily, and with it in all probability will be offered the friendship that boat owners always seem to feel towards one another.

Cherish that friendship. Lend a hand whenever someone else is hauling up their boat, or is trying to untangle a particularly stubborn fishing line. But don't expect profuse thanks for your assistance, for such small acts of courtesy are taken for granted on practically every beach. Your thanks will come later, in a more practical form, when you also are in need of a helping hand.

Although the B.B.C. broadcast detailed weather forecasts several times a day, it is nevertheless advisable that every owner of a small boat should be able to read Nature's weather signs. During the course of a day's fishing trip several miles offshore one is cut off from the official forecasts for many hours, and may thus remain blissfully ignorant of the fact that a gale warning has been issued. For those unversed in weather lore such a situation could—and all too often does—end in disaster. Yet rarely does a dangerous shift or rise in the wind come without any warning signs whatever, and from the appearance of the clouds and the behaviour of sea birds experienced sailors are able to tell that something is brewing well in advance. It is a case then of 'up-killick and make for the shore', for under the influence of a strong wind an ugly sea can spring up in a matter of minutes.

Dawn, a popular time for fishing, is a notoriously tricky time so far as the weather is concerned. A flat calm may be on the sea as the sun rises, and an hour later a really stiff breeze may be blowing, with white-capped combers piling up on the shore, making it decidedly unpleasant to land in a small boat.

The wind also has a habit of 'backing' round about dawn, which is the term used when the wind swings round 'against the sun'. A backing wind is often extremely unstable; or, as West Country fishermen say:

> When the wind do shift agin the sun,
> Trust un not, f'r back 'twill run.

Consequently, sailing craft often make use of this backing dawn wind to reach a fishing ground, in the well-founded belief that it will 'veer' (swing round with the sun) again in time to assist them on the return trip.

As may be expected, the weather rhymes relating to the various types of dawn are numerous; perhaps the best known being:

> Red sky in the morning,
> Sailor take warning.

Another version goes even further:

> Sunset red and morning grey,
> Are certain signs of a beautiful day.
> But an evening grey and a morning red
> Will make any sailor shake his head.

Both these old rhymes are surprisingly reliable, and are, indeed, backed up by solid scientific facts. Another piece of traditional weather wisdom declares that when the first vestiges of dawnlight appear above a bank of cloud the day that follows will be windy. Fishermen refer to this as a 'high dawn'. A 'low dawn', on the other hand—with the sun first appearing below any cloud formations—is an indication of settled conditions.

No boat fisherman should set off on a dawn fishing trip without first giving his barometer a glance, if he has one. If it has fallen overnight to any marked extent a change for the worse in the weather may be expected, with wind and rain. Conversely, a barometer rises for cold, dry and less wind.

There are two more rhymes which should be remembered when consulting the glass:

> Long foretold, long last;
> Short foretold, soon past.

and

> First rise after very low
> Foretells a stronger blow.

Remember, too, to take heed of any very rapid rise of the barometer; it may well indicate squally weather. A slow rise is always to be preferred; it is almost always a sign of settled conditions.

Cloud formations are excellent weather indicators, and reading them comes as second nature to most people who live by the sea. Soft, round, fleecy-looking clouds do not occasion the sailor much concern as they rarely accompany strong winds—although they may grow into rain clouds. On the other hand, long, ragged clouds of the sort known as mares' tails are well-known harbingers of wind, and the equally familiar mackerel sky is also to be distrusted.

> Mackerel sky and mares' tails,
> Make tall ships carry low sails.

Also:

> Mackerel sky—
> Never long wet; nor yet long dry.

One of the most certain indications of really wet weather to come, however, is given by an unusually clear atmosphere. Distant objects appear to be quite close at hand, and often a lambent glow seems to suffuse the whole seascape. At such times sounds carry for surprising distances; a spray of mackerel may be heard breaking the surface a mile away; or, maybe, the thudding exhaust of a diesel craft will make itself heard before the boat itself has appeared round a distant headland.

While on the subject of wet weather, there is another little rhyme to help one memorise the relationship between wind and rain:

> When rain comes before the wind,
> Halyards, sheets and braces mind.
> When wind arrives before the rain,
> You'll soon be making sail again.

GALE WARNINGS

Apart from the gale warnings broadcast by the B.B.C. visual warnings are hoisted at numerous points all round the coast for the benefit of small craft without radio receiving sets. These signals take the form of a large black cone during the day, or lights arranged in a triangle by night. They take two forms: North Cones and South Cones.

North Cones are hoisted point upwards, indicating that in that particular area a gale is imminent, and is expected from the north; or, alternatively, from the east or west, afterwards swinging round towards the north.

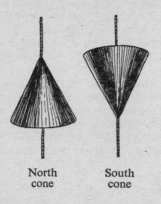

North   South
cone   cone

South Cones are hoisted point downwards, indicating that the approaching gale is expected to commence from a southerly point; possibly backing later through east to north-east. South cones are also hoisted for gales commencing from either east or west, and afterwards swinging round towards the south.

FOG

There is nothing more bewildering to the occupants of a small boat than the sudden descent of a thick fog, and under certain conditions it is possible—unless precautions are taken immediately—to become completely lost when only half a mile or so offshore.

When a fog bank is seen approaching one should immediately begin to make for the nearest land, at the same time noting the set of the waves, direction of the wind and position of the sun; each of which may be of assistance later in keeping the boat on her course. Unfortunately, it is a fact that fog at sea is often accompanied by a flat calm and a complete absence of wind, and when really thick not even a slight lightening in the vapour overhead will provide any hint as to the position of the sun. Unless a compass is carried—as it certainly ought to be—one is almost sure to become lost under such conditions.

The safest course to adopt when lost in a fog is to drop anchor and wait for the visibility to improve; or, if you know yourself to be near the shore, to rest on your oars (or cut off the motor) and listen for any sounds drifting across from the land. If near a shipping lane, give audible warning of your presence at least once every minute by banging on an empty tin, if you have one in the boat. This noise, augmented by occasional loud shouts, may bring an answering hail from the shore. Once contact has been made with the shore in this way it should be possible to head slowly back to base.

If you are completely lost, and contact cannot be made with the shore, do not hesitate to anchor. Even though the boat may appear to be motionless when you are resting on your oars, it will be drifting along with the tide all the while. By the time the fog lifts you may be miles from the place you started from, and possibly a very long way from land. Needless to say, an anchor should always be carried in the boat as a safety precaution; but if you do happen to be without one you may, with luck, be able to hitch on to a lobster-pot rope, or a buoy.

There are certain 'rules of the road' at sea which should be known by every boat owner. They are as follows:

1. A vessel proceeding under sail always has the right of way over power-driven craft.

2. A sailing boat that is running free should keep out of the way of a sailing boat that is close-hauled.

3. When two sailing boats are approaching each other from opposite directions, both of them close-hauled, the one on the port tack (i.e. with the wind blowing on to her port side) should keep out of the way of the one on the starboard tack.

4. When two sailing boats are running free, with the wind on different sides, the boat which has the wind on the port side should steer clear of the other.

5. When two sailing boats are running free, with the wind on the same side, the boat which is to windward should steer clear of the one to leeward.

6. When two power-driven boats are approaching bows on to one another each should change course to starboard. At night this would mean that they would pass with their port (red) navigation lights nearest each other.

7. When two boats are approaching in opposite directions, but starboard to starboard, or port to port, both should maintain their course and speed. A sailors' rhyme treats the subject as follows:

> Green light to green light ; red to red,
> Perfect safety—go ahead.

8. When two power-driven boats are crossing, the boat which is showing her port side to the other has the right of way. If necessary, the other must change her course, halt, or slow down and pass astern.

9. A boat being overtaken maintains her course and speed. It is the duty of the other boat to keep clear.

10. All craft, large or small, are expected to keep well clear of fishing vessels and their gear—nets, lines, etc.

11. Small boats should never argue over the right of way with large ocean-going vessels, especially in confined waters. A rowing boat is far more manœuvrable than a liner, and it is simpler—and a lot safer—for it to keep clear.

12. At night, rowing boats, whether under oars or sail, should carry a lantern or electric flashlamp, so that it may be temporarily exhibited when other craft are in the vicinity.

BUOYS

Buoys are the traffic signs of the sea, and are most commonly used to indicate the direction of a harbour entrance or navigable channel. They are of three main shapes, and bear corresponding names: conical, can and spherical.

Conical Buoys (*a*) show a pointed top, and are painted either black or black and white chequered. They should always be kept to starboard (*see* important 'note' below). Sometimes, in order to make it easier for them to be sighted from a distance, they are surmounted by a staff and black cone.

NOTE: By 'starboard' in this instance is meant the right-hand side of craft ascending a river or estuary, or proceeding in the direction of the main flood-tide along the coast.

Can Buoys (*b*) have flat tops, and are painted either red or red and white chequered. They should always be kept to port (*see* important 'note' below). Sometimes they are surmounted by a staff and red can.

NOTE: By 'port' in this instance is meant the left-hand side of craft ascending a river or estuary, or proceeding in the direction of the main flood-tide along the coast.

Spherical Buoys (*c*) show a domed top, and serve to indicate the ends of 'middle grounds', as obstructions to the entrances to harbours and channels are called. When the main channel lies to the right the buoy is painted with red

and white horizontal bands, whilst sometimes an outer buoy
is surmounted by a staff and red can, and an inner one by a
staff and red 'T'. When the channels are of equal importance
the buoys are painted in the same way, but sometimes the
outer one is surmounted by a staff and red sphere, and the
inner one by a staff and red St. George's cross. When the
main channel lies to the left buoys are painted with black
and white horizontal stripes ; an outer one sometimes being

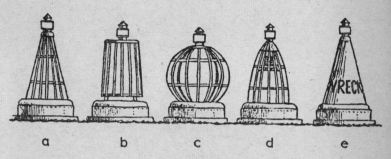

BUOYS
(see text for description and use)

surmounted by a staff and black cone, and an inner one by a
staff and black diamond.

Apart from the types of buoy mentioned above, there
are others which are used to mark the positions of special
navigational hazards, such as reefs, sands, wrecks, etc. Many
of these carry bells, whistles or lights.

Bell Buoys (*d*) are worked by the rocking motion caused
by the waves.

Whistling Buoys are also operated by wave motion, only
in their case the up-and-down movement of the buoy works
a bellows, which drives spasmodic gusts of air through the
whistle.

Light Buoys, as a rule, are operated by a store of com-
pressed gas contained inside the buoy itself ; although some,
situated mostly in river estuaries, are worked by electricity

brought from the shore by underwater cable. Many conical, can and spherical buoys carry lights.

Wreck Buoys (e) are painted green, and bear the word 'WRECK'. Sometimes they exhibit a flashing green light at night. They may be can-shaped (to be passed on the port hand), conical (starboard hand) or spherical (pass on either hand).

Part I—The Tides

Apart from keeping himself conversant with the varying daily times of high and low water, there are a number of other facts concerning the tides which every person living by the sea should know.

As most people are aware, the periodical rising and falling of the sea's surface is caused by the attractions of the moon and sun. The tide-producing power of the moon is rather more than twice as great as that of the sun, and it is this difference between the 'pull' of the sun and that of the moon that is directly responsible for the phenomena known as spring and neap tides.

Spring Tides occur at new and full moon, when both moon and sun are exerting their powers of attraction on the same areas of ocean. It is at such times that the highest and lowest tides are experienced all round the world as the earth revolves, and the 'tide-bulge' reaches every sea and ocean in turn.

Neap Tides occur when the moon is either at the first or last quarter. At these periods the attractive powers of the moon and the sun oppose each other by pulling at different areas of ocean, with the result that the rise and fall of the tides is reduced to a minimum. (*See* diagram overleaf.)

Rising and falling tides are said to 'flow' and 'ebb', and this term is also used in connection with the currents which, in shallow waters, are a direct result of the rise and fall of the ocean. In many places the flowing and ebbing of these currents 'over-run' the actual times of high and low water on the adjacent shore ; frequently by as much as three hours or more. Thus, at high and low water on the shore the tidal currents are often running at their maximum speed.

The duration of this period of over-running is one of the

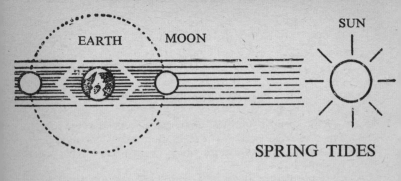

EARTH · MOON · SUN

SPRING TIDES

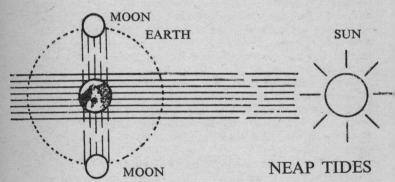

MOON · EARTH · SUN

MOON

NEAP TIDES

In the top illustration the moon is at the full and new positions respectively. In the lower illustration the moon is shown in the first and last quarter positions

(*See text for explanation*)

first things which should be ascertained by anyone using a boat on an unfamiliar stretch of coast. In this respect, personal observation or reference to a chart is far more reliable than hearsay, and the best method of judging the strength and direction of the current is to anchor the boat for a few seconds and cast some small buoyant object overboard and watch its speed of drift. Alternatively, the boat may be allowed to drift past some fixed object, such as a lobster-pot cork.

This precaution is not unnecessary. Tidal currents with a maximum velocity of several knots are quite common around the coasts of Britain, and at spring tides a small rowing boat can easily get into difficulties among them, especially if there is a headwind to be contended with at the same time. Tide races are usually strongest and most turbulent off headlands where the water is shoaly, and opposing currents meet. However, dangerous currents also sweep in and out of many bays and river estuaries; often flowing directly over rocks and shoals.

The rise and fall of the tides varies considerably around the British Isles. On the east coast of Ireland the average range amounts to only two feet; along the western reaches of the English Channel about ten feet would probably be nearer the mark; whilst at Bristol a range of no less than fifty feet has been recorded at spring tides. The time between each high tide averages out at about 12 hrs. 25½ mins.; but for reasons too complicated to be dealt with here this period does not remain constant. At the period of springs the tides arrive early, or 'prime', and the interval between high waters is only about 12 hrs. 19 mins. At neap tides, on the other hand, the tides arrive late, or 'lag', with an interval between them of approximately 12 hrs. 33 mins.

Finally, it should be realised that winds can affect the normal behaviour of the tides to a considerable extent. A gale blowing in the same direction as a tide can cause an abnormally long flow, whilst a gale opposing a tide can reduce its range by many feet.

Part II—Waves and Swell

Sea waves are normally caused by the friction of wind blowing over the surface of the water, and their motion has been compared to those undulations which pass along a rope when it is shaken. Just as the waves 'flow' along the rope without imparting any forward motion to the rope itself, so does the water comprising a series of sea waves remain stationary while the undulations on the surface rush forward under the influence of the wind.

Such, at any rate, is the behaviour of waves in the open sea. When waves reach shallow water, however, they are 'tripped up', forming surf-crested breakers that are capable of hurling themselves against a solid body, such as a rock, sea-wall, or boat, with great force.

Scientists have devoted much time to the study of sea waves, and it has been found that shortly after waves are formed the ratio between their height (vertical distance between trough and crest) and length (distance between crest and crest) is approximately 1 to 12. The maximum theoretical steepness is also given as being 1 in 7, but the writer suspects that there are many sailors who will feel convinced that they have had personal dealings with waves far steeper than this.

The speed at which waves travel depends upon their size, and giant waves have been observed in mid-ocean travelling at over 80 miles per hour. Such waves would have to be accompanied by a gale of exceptional severity, however, and the chances are that their gradient would only amount to about 1 in 25, as waves normally become less steep as their speed increases.

At the peak of a prolonged storm in mid-ocean the maximum height and length of the waves may be computed by estimating the velocity of the wind in knots, and multiplying this figure by itself. The result of this calculation should then be divided by 50 to obtain the height of the waves in feet, and by 2 to obtain their length, also in feet. The actual heights of storm waves in mid-ocean are very difficult to measure with any degree of accuracy, but it has been estimated that, in the Atlantic, storms producing 50-foot waves occur two or three times every year; whilst 80-foot waves have been witnessed on occasions.

It should be realised that, in a storm, many smaller and steeper waves will be travelling over the surface of these large waves, and it is this combination which helps to make a really ugly sea. For instance, when a small vessel, riding a wave with a gradient of 1 in 20, suddenly encounters another short, breaking wave with a pitch of 1 in 7, the situation may easily prove critical.

Large storm waves will travel across the surface of an ocean for many days after the wind which originally formed them has died away. Their surface, however, becomes unruffled by smaller waves in a comparatively short time, and these long, smooth waves are then referred to as a 'swell'. It has been computed that swell waves lose about a third of their height whilst travelling the same number of miles as they measure, in feet, from crest to crest. In other words, 27-foot-high waves, measuring 600 feet from crest to crest, will still be 18 feet high after travelling 600 miles; 12 feet high after 1,200 miles, and 8 feet high after 1,800 miles. Should these swell waves encounter an opposing wind at some point along their course, however, they would lose height more rapidly.

In the open sea a swell is never dangerous to a seaworthy boat, but on coasts exposed to a wide reach of ocean it can make the launching and beaching of a small boat an extremely tricky operation. Swell also has to be taken into consideration when fishing or prawning close to rocks; for although the motion of a long 5-foot swell is scarcely noticeable, the descent of a boat from that height on to a jagged rock is quite sufficient to put a hole through its timbers.

Men have always feared and respected the sea—that 'old grey widow-maker', as Kipling so aptly describes it. For when a man goes to sea in a boat he leaves his own element behind, and puts himself at the mercy of the deep, restless salt water, and the craft in which he sails. To the sailor, the sea and his boat are both living things, and because of this he has, since the very earliest of times, taken good care to avoid offending either of them in any way.

The sea especially has always had a nasty temper, and the mariner of old used to try to appease its wrath by offering a sacrifice to it whenever a new boat was launched for the first time. The idea has persisted down the long centuries, and today the sacrifice consists of breaking a bottle of champagne over the bows of the vessel at its christening ceremony. But there is evidence to indicate that, thousands of years ago, the boats of our distant seafaring ancestors were blessed, not with any form of wine, but with the still warm blood of a freshly killed human being. The unfortunate victim of the ritual was beheaded, and his head impaled in a prominent position on the bows or stern of the boat, so that the Sea God would be sure to notice its presence there with approval.

As the people around these coasts gradually grew more sea-minded, so the numbers of boats—and victims—increased. Eventually, presumably when the supply of victims had been used up, some bold boat-owner played rather a mean trick on the God of the Sea. He fashioned a mop-like object from some old pieces of rope and stuck that on his boat instead of the customary human head. Apparently the Sea God was easily hoodwinked, for no black storm arose to engulf him on his first fishing trip, and after a while others began to follow his example. Thousands of years passed, but still mariners continued to protect themselves against the wrath of the sea with this ruse. Around our shores the imitation heads became more and more elaborate, until in fairly recent times the bunch of ropes-ends gave way to the beautifully carved wooden figureheads which graced the full-rigged clipper ships of the last century. These figureheads, like many another link with the superstitious seafarers of old, have now been ousted by the marine engine. Yet the more primitive mop-like head may still be seen on fishing boats around the Mediterranean, Spanish and Portuguese

Carved wooden figurehead
from a full-rigged clipper

coasts. In Britain, too, it is believed that the tradition persists among those brightly decorated canal barges known as narrow boats. For the rudder posts of these craft are frequently adorned with an elaborately coiled and plaited length of pipe-clayed rope, which the boatmen refer to as a 'turk's head'.

The lives of sailors have always been complicated by the belief that a thoughtless act, or a carelessly uttered word, could bring bad luck in its wake. Since time immemorial no right-minded person has dreamed of launching a new vessel on a Friday, and this taboo is still observed in quite a number of modern shipyards. It was also considered unlucky to set sail on a Friday, and only the other day I heard of an instance where the owners of a new motor collier, at the urgent request of the crew, delayed for twenty-four hours the vessel's maiden voyage, which was to have commenced on a Friday.

Just why Friday should be regarded by sailors as a day of ill-omen must remain a matter for conjecture; although, like many superstitions of the sea, it probably originated abroad. Ever since Phoenician traders first came to our shores to barter for Cornish tin, there has been a constant exchange of maritime ideas and beliefs between our seamen and those of the Mediterranean. It is, perhaps, significant that the Muslims who inhabit the southern shores of the Mediterranean consider Friday to be a day quite out of the ordinary. They believe, for instance, that Adam was created and received into paradise on a Friday; that Friday was the day he was expelled from it, the day on which he repented, and the day on which he died. They also believe that the day of general resurrection will take place on a Friday. Small wonder, then, that the superstitious sailors of long ago avoided putting to sea on a day when such startling things were liable to happen!

As everyone knows, a ship or a boat is always referred to as 'she', and many people are apt to wonder why this should be. The most likely explanation is that the sailor of old, believing that the deity of the sea was a man, began referring to his boat as a woman in the hope that the Sea God would be moved by feelings of chivalry to treat his craft more kindly. From this belief that his boat was a member of the fair sex there arose several other sailors' superstitions of great antiquity. Very widely held was the belief that it was unlucky to have a woman on a ship. A sailor could have a girl in every port and no harm was likely to result; but to put to sea with a woman on board was simply courting disaster. It is not difficult to see how this superstition arose. The vessel, being a woman, would become jealous of any competition from her own sex, and from then onwards would never rest content until she had vented her spite on the crew.

Naturally, with the advent of the modern passenger liner

this superstition was bound to die a natural death; although traces of it can still be found amongst some longshore fishing communities. In remote parts of Ireland, for instance, the men will on no account take a woman out on a fishing trip, lest her presence in the boat should result in a poor catch.

A number of our sailors' superstitions were doubtless brought to the shores of Britain by the Romans. Neptune, for instance, was originally a much-feared and respected Roman god who had complete power over the wind and the waves. It paid the sailors of olden times to keep on the right side of him, and when a storm was threatening certain prayers and incantations were offered up to him, even by sailors who quite honestly believed themselves to be devout Christians. Those sailors would have been horrified at our present-day light-hearted attitude towards 'King' Neptune, and would certainly never recognise him in the genial Old Man of the Sea, who comes scrambling over the side of the modern luxury liner as she crosses the Equator.

Just as the art of longshore fishing is older than that of deep-water sailing, so do the superstitions and rituals observed by Britain's longshoremen tend to have a longer pedigree than those of her foreign-going mariners. Many longshore beliefs, in fact, date from pre-Roman times, and from their nature it seems likely that they owe much to the influence of the ancient Druid priesthood. For instance, until only a few years ago, the longshore fishermen of West Dorset used to hang a stone with a naturally formed hole through its middle to the stemposts of their boats. This was done to ensure good catches of fish—for there was a widespread belief that a stone shaped like this was lucky.

Now this was pure Celtic wizardry. Those readers who have toured Devon and Cornwall may have seen some of those West Country megalithic remains known as 'quoits', which are, in fact, nothing more than huge stones with a hole through the middle. One of the best known in Cornwall is Men-an-Tol, in the westernmost peninsula of the county. There can be little doubt that such stones were venerated by the pagan priesthood, who believed that they contained supernatural powers of considerable benefit to the community. Lovers plighted their troth by linking hands through the hole in the stone ; cripples thrust their diseased limbs into the aperture to be cured ; weakly babes were passed through the opening to be made strong again.

Thousands of years have now passed since the Druids held their mystic rites, but these hoary stones are still visited by cripples seeking health, and lovers in search of happiness. True, these 'pagan pilgrimages' are not so numerous as they were until about fifty years ago, but they are a lot more common than many people would suppose.

But let us return to the sea-shore. Many children—and grown-ups, too—hasten to pick up any stone they chance to see on the beach which has a naturally formed hole through its centre. They spit through this hole for 'luck', and then cast it away over their left shoulder. Few who indulge in this now almost meaningless custom realise that they are perpetuating a rite which may well be linked with the blood sacrifices of the pagan Druid priesthood.

Another belief of our heathen ancestors was that certain actions were extremely unlucky when performed widdershins—that is to say, when made in the opposite direction to that taken by the sun as it moves across the heavens. Until recent times, no longshore fisherman would turn his boat round on the beach against the sun. Some of the older fishermen in the Celtic west still observe this custom, although it is doubtful if any realise that in doing so they are unconsciously paying obeisance to the Sun God, which at one time played almost as important a part in the lives of their ancestors as the God of the Sea. These old West Country fishermen only know that when they turn a boat widdershins 'it do seem all wrong'.

Two or three hundred years ago there were few people, landsmen or seamen, who did not have a healthy fear of witchcraft. Among the many evil accomplishments that a witch was supposed to possess was the ability to change herself into the form of her 'familiar'. A witch's familiar was usually some animal, such as a rabbit, hare, goat, pig, cat or fox. The fishermen of those times, by virtue of the dangerous nature of their calling, were so afraid of attracting the attention of a witch that they would not even mention one of these creatures in the course of their conversation. The taboo on these words lasted long after this country ceased to believe in witchcraft, and only a few years ago in the Cornish fishing harbour of Looe, I heard of an instance when this unwritten law was unwittingly broken. One day, so my informant told me, some of the local fishermen were preserving their nets by dipping them in boiling tar when they were approached by a local vermin trapper.

'Good day,' the trapper greeted them. 'I was wondering whether you'd do me a favour?'

'That all depends,' one of the fishermen replied, cautiously. 'Tell us what 'ee wants us to do first.'

'Well,' said the trapper, producing a bundle. 'I was wondering if you'd dip these for me while you're tarring your own nets. It'll only take you a minute. They're just a few old rabbit nets.'

For a moment the fishermen stared at the trapper in shocked silence; then with an angry roar they rushed forward and pitched the bewildered man out of the shed. He had uttered the forbidden word 'rabbit', and he had paid the penalty!

There are other words which the sailor regards as unlucky, and not so very long ago it was almost as much as a person's life was worth to mention salt to a fisherman. Perhaps it was associated in his mind with the salt water that was always waiting to claim him. Similarly, to fisherman and deep-sea sailor alike, a parson has always been a symbol of ill-fortune. To utter the word 'parson' out loud is bad enough, but to have one on board your ship or boat is even worse. Doubtless this is yet another superstition that goes back to the days when sailors went in constant fear of arousing the Sea God's displeasure. For what was more likely to bring about this jealous deity's wrath than to have a representative of the God of Heaven invading his own watery domain?

Indeed, there were once so many ways in which a sailor could accidentally conjure up a storm and disaster that to some people it must seem remarkable that any lived to become grizzled old salts. Fortunately, however, the accidental breaking of a taboo could usually be remedied by spitting. Perhaps that is why, even to this day, sailors are so adept at the art of expectoration!

Not only did the mariner himself have to be constantly on his guard against falling foul of these superstitions of the sea ; it was also necessary for his womenfolk to watch what they were about. Most of their fears were connected in some way with symbolical acts. For instance, a loaf placed upside-down on the table put them in mind of a capsized boat, and made them fear for the safety of their bread-winner. By a similar thought process, an umbrella opened indoors was liable to call up such a tempest that even a stoutly built cottage would not give one sufficient shelter from its ruthless blast. What hope then for their unfortunate menfolk, who would be far out at sea when the storm broke?

No fisherman liked to hear his wife whistling ; the sound was too reminiscent of a gale in the rigging for his peace of mind. The men, too, refrained from whistling whilst at sea ; although sometimes, when they were becalmed, the skipper might try to persuade a breeze to blow their way by whistling very softly and gently. But even then he would be careful to whistle only in the direction from which he wished the breeze to blow.

A custom observed on board ship which often puzzles the landsman is that of ringing the ship's bell at certain intervals. He knows, of course, that it is the seaman's method of keeping track of the time, but he cannot help feeling that it is all rather complicated and unnecessary. There is, perhaps, some truth in this ; although few sailors would be willing to admit it. The fact remains, however, that bells were not originally hung on board ship for the purpose of telling the time, or changing the watch. Instead, they were used to frighten away evil spirits, and to dispel storms. The fact that, for safety's sake, the bells were rung at regular intervals was purely incidental.

Nowadays a ship's bell is regarded with affection rather than veneration, but it is significant perhaps that it is one of the few things that are neither sold nor broken up when a vessel's sea-going days are over. Usually it is presented to someone who had a special interest in the ship; such as the skipper who last commanded her.

Since time immemorial there have been both lucky and unlucky ships. The Royal Navy has long recognised this fact, and those vessels which are fortunate or victorious in battle are almost invariably succeeded by others of the same name. For instance at the time of writing four ships have borne the name of *Ark Royal*.

The first *Ark Royal* was a ship of 800 tons burthen, which, in 1588, assisted in the defeat of the Spanish Armada, carrying the flag of the Lord Admiral of the Fleet. During the Second World War the narrow escapes of the third *Ark Royal*, a 22,000-ton aircraft carrier, took on an almost legendary character, and for a while she was known as the luckiest ship in the Royal Navy. Time and time again the Germans thought they had sunk her, and early in the war a German airman called Francke received special promotion and a letter of congratulation from Goering for bombing and 'sinking' her in the North Sea. The enemy were therefore not a little ruffled when, in May 1941, aircraft of the *Ark Royal* played a major part in the destruction of their own 'unsinkable' battleship, the *Bismarck*, which was on its first ocean voyage.

Later on, the *Ark Royal* operated in that notorious 'hot-spot' of the war, the Mediterranean, inflicting considerable damage on the Italian Navy and the Regia Aeronautica. Eventually she was torpedoed by a German submarine; but although doomed, her reputation for being a lucky ship held good, for she remained afloat for nearly twelve hours, and only one man was lost. It is not surprising, therefore, that the Admiralty have perpetuated the memory of the *Ark Royal* by building another £20,000,000 aircraft carrier of the same name.

Fortunately, there have not been many unlucky warships in the Royal Navy. The worst offender on record was H.M.S. *Camperdown*, a 10,600-ton battleship, launched in 1885. According to many sailors who served in her, she brought bad luck to her crew from the very beginning; but it was not until 1893 that matters reached their climax. Then, while on manœuvres in the Mediterranean, the *Camperdown* suddenly altered course and rammed her companion ship, H.M.S. *Victoria,* with the loss of hundreds of lives. The disaster was one of the worst ever to befall the Navy in peacetime, and how it ever came to occur has remained a mystery to this day. The only person who could have given an explanation was the commander of the *Camperdown,* and he went down with his ship. Needless to say, no other unit of the Royal Navy has since borne the name of this ill-starred vessel.

To the superstitious sailor it sometimes appears as though a ship is more than unlucky; she seems to be harbouring some malignant hatred for all who sail in her. Consider for a moment the case of the *Great Eastern,* which was conceived in 1852 by Isambard Kingdom Brunel, an engineering genius who had already played a leading role in various remarkable achievements, such as the construction of the Great Western Railway and the Rotherhithe Tunnel, and the designing of the Clifton Suspension Bridge. His 22,500-ton *Great Eastern* was a daring project; she was to be larger than any ship so far built, and powered both by paddles and a screw. Yet from the very day her keel-plate was laid down this 692-foot monster seemed to bring disaster to all who handled her. When she was launched at Millwall, in 1858, six men had already met their deaths while building her, and rumour had it that the evilly disposed vessel had also killed two others, a riveter and his boy. But in spite of a search their bodies could not be found.

The *Great Eastern* sailed on her maiden voyage on September 7th, 1859, and a week later her designer also died. Almost at the same time the ship was shaken by a terrific explosion, which killed another fifteen men, and the trip across the Atlantic had to be postponed. Not until the following year, in fact, did this 'blood-thirsty giantess'—as sailors were already calling her—eventually reach New York. On this voyage she succeeded in drowning two of her crew, whilst another was found dead in his bunk.

On a return passage to England she ran into a great storm

and almost foundered when her paddle-wheels and steering gear were put out of action. The captain got her into Cork harbour, but even there she managed to kill yet another member of the crew—the quartermaster—with a sudden back-kick of her helm.

By this time the owners of the *Great Eastern* were already troubled by an uneasy suspicion that she was going to prove a financial failure. These doubts were confirmed later on when she tried to commit hara-kiri by tearing herself wide open on an uncharted rock off Long Island. Not without difficulty the damage was patched up, and there was some talk then about selling her to the Sultan of Turkey as a sea-going pleasure palace for his numerous wives.

Instead, from 1865 onwards, she was employed in laying telegraph cables across the Atlantic, and in the Mediterranean and Red Seas. But her reputation for being a thoroughly evil-natured ship remained until she was sold for scrap in 1888. Even the £58,000 that the ship-breakers paid for her seemed to be an echo of her unlucky history, for there were plenty of people who noted, without much surprise, that this sum was exactly one-thirteenth of her original cost.

Why was the *Great Eastern* so unlucky? The ship-breakers thought they had found the answer when they began to strip the plates from the outside of her hull. For there, trapped inside the ship's double shell, they came upon two mildewed and rat-gnawed skeletons; a man's and a child's. At first the discovery was a mystery to all concerned; until someone remembered the riveter and his lad who had mysteriously disappeared some thirty-odd years before, while helping to build the ship.

It is impossible to delve among the fascinating legends of the sea without being confronted, sooner or later, with strange tales of ghost ships. Most famous of these phantom vessels is, of course, the *Flying Dutchman*, which is reputed to haunt that part of the Indian Ocean which lies off the Cape of Good Hope. The story goes that a certain Captain Van der Decken, outward bound from Europe to the Far East, found himself delayed off the Cape for week after week by contrary winds. Eventually his passengers and crew asked him to put about to Table Bay, where they would be able to wait in security and comfort for more favourable weather conditions. The captain, however, swore with a profane and terrible oath that if he could not make any easting he would continue to beat back and forth until the Day of Judgement. No sooner were the words out of his mouth than the wind increased to hurricane force, and giant seas arose, sweeping the crew and passengers overboard. Only the captain remained at the helm, doomed to fulfil the blasphemous promise he had uttered in anger. And to this day, so many old seamen declare, the *Flying Dutchman* may yet be seen beating back and forth off the southern coast of Africa, with storm-tattered sails set on splintered masts, and with the gaunt figure of Captain Van der Decken still grimly standing at the helm.

Just an old seaman's yarn, you may say with a smile ; and you are probably right. Yet every so often strange things happen in those waters which are apt to make some people wonder whether there might not be more in the story than they at first supposed. During the Second World War, when I was serving with an R.A.F. squadron stationed near the Cape of Good Hope, a lifeboat filled with survivors from a torpedoed merchantman was washed ashore on a lonely stretch of nearby coast. These seamen declared that, while drifting one night in their lifeboat, they had sighted the *Flying Dutchman*. She had appeared quite clearly in bright, near-tropical moonlight as a two-masted, square-rigged ship, and at first they had seen nothing unusual about her, except that she seemed rather old-fashioned. But as soon as they had hailed her, confident that she would heave to and pick them up, she vanished into thin air.

The sceptics, of course, declared that this was an obvious case of mass hallucination, resulting from thirst and exposure. To such criticism it is almost impossible to find an answer. Yet, if such things as ghost ships do not exist, how can one explain the following entry in the official log of H.M.S. *Bacchante,* recorded during the latter half of the last century?

'At 4 a.m. she crossed our bows. A strange, red light, as of a phantom ship all aglow, in the midst of which light the broken masts, spars and torn sails of a brig, 200 yards distant, stood out in strong relief as she came up with us.

'The look-out man on our fo'c'sle reported her as close to the port bow, where also the officer of the watch from the bridge clearly saw her, as did the quarter-deck midshipman, who was sent forward at once to the fo'c'sle, but on arriving there no vestige, nor any sign whatever of any material ship could be seen.'

It is interesting to note that a young cadet aboard H.M.S. *Bacchante* requested permission to copy this entry into his personal diary. He was the late King George the Fifth, who at the time was serving in the warship as a midshipman.

There have always been ships which possessed a reputation for being haunted, and a well-authenticated case of this kind was that of the liner *Utopia*. Outward bound from Italy, she collided with H.M.S. *Anson* in Gibraltar Bay, and at once began to settle in the water. Frantic efforts were made by the liner's crew to save all the passengers, but when the vessel plunged to the bottom she took with her a large number of men and women who had become lost and trapped inside her.

Eventually the sunken liner was brought to the surface again by a salvage company and towed to harbour. There, in dry dock, she was repaired and refitted, and afterwards returned to service. But as soon as she was afloat again strange things began to happen aboard the resurrected liner, and whenever she passed Gibraltar Bay eerie sounds were heard by officers, crew and passengers. Many said that these noises resembled the last agonised cries of drowning men and women. Not surprisingly, therefore, the ship's passenger list dwindled with every trip, and the owners experienced considerable difficulty in finding seamen willing to sail in her. So, although still modern and well-found, she was sent to the breakers' yard.

John Masefield, in writing of an old-time sailing ship,

described her as being 'of great beauty but strange dooms'. When penning those lines he might well have been thinking of an American schooner called the *Star,* which tempted fate one day by putting to sea with a crew of thirteen. Off Midway Island, in the Pacific Ocean, she ran into bad weather and piled herself up on a submerged reef. Her condition seemed so hopeless that the crew took to their boat, and were lucky enough to be picked up by a passing barque, which in due course put them ashore near Seattle, on the west coast of the United States.

Everyone had more or less forgotten about the loss of the *Star* when, six months later, the captain of a vessel called the *Doon* reported seeing the schooner out on the open Pacific, well distant from the position where she had foundered. Her sails were expertly set, and she was sailing fast to windward. There was no question of it being a case of mistaken identity, for the two ships had passed close to each other, and visibility had been perfect.

Three months later the *Star* was again reported, this time by an oil tanker, which gave her position as being 400 miles west of San Francisco. Thus, the schooner had by this time travelled well over 2,000 miles from the reef on which she had come to grief. Moreover, the tanker reported that she was sailing under full sail, and everything about her appeared to be in perfect order.

The *Star* now seems to have altered course and sailed away from the American coast in a south-westerly direction, for she was next sighted off Fanning Island, a small British possession in the middle of the Pacific. This made her about 3,000 miles from her last reported position; so that since leaving the place where she had been abandoned, she must have sailed something like 5,000 miles. During this time she had eluded several ships that had been despatched specially to intercept her and bring her back to port, and at Fanning Island she ignored signals from a cable ship and a shore signals station.

Still maintaining her south-westerly course, the *Star* steered her way amongst several coral atolls, until she reached Hull Island, in the Phoenix group. By that time she had logged

Young gulls circling offshore

The sign of approaching rain—NIMBUS cloud formation

LANGUAGE OF THE SKY

Low Clouds with bases below 7,000 feet	CUMULUS (i)	Dense masses with edges sharply defined or like huge puffs of smoke	Stormy or showers
	CUMULUS (ii)	Banks of soft white cloud	Fine weather
	STRATUS	Sheet cloud resembling fog	Fine weather
	NIMBUS	Ugly ragged clouds or a low amorphous rainy layer of dark grey	Rainstorm usually accompanied by high wind
High Clouds with bases above 20,000 feet	CIRRUS	Delicate detached, fibrous texture clouds	Fair weather
	CIRRO-CUMULUS	Small globular whitish masses in lines or ripples developing sometimes to Alto-cumulus, also arranged in groups, lines or rolls	Neutral
Middle Clouds with bases between 8,000-20,000 feet	ALTO-STRATUS	Thick sheet of grey or bluish colour showing a brilliant patch in the vicinity of the sun or moon sometimes develops from Cirro-Stratus—a thin white sheet covering the whole sky	Rain approaching

The CUMULO-NIMBUS cloud formation above, with its characteristic
mountainous mass invariably indicates showers
or thunderstorm

Another forerunner of rain: CIRRO-STRATUS with FRACTO-CUMULUS

CUMULUS CLOUDS gathering in the glory of high summer; usually these clouds indicate fine settled weather, but when they grow in vertical extent look out for showers

another 1,000 miles, and was fast becoming a legend—a veritable *Flying Dutchman* of the Pacific. Sailors who had caught sight of the schooner swore solemnly that they had seen men aboard her, dressed in the sort of clothes worn by seafarers in the days of Elizabeth the First. Some said they were the phantom crew of a vessel that had been wrecked hundreds of years before on the reef that had ensnared the *Star*. These phantoms, they declared, had risen from the deep when the schooner struck, and had gone a-roving in her once more. There were others, of course, who protested that such theories were fantastic.

But if there was nothing supernatural about that schooner how can we explain away what eventually happened to her? The Pacific Ocean covers an area of 70,000,000 square miles, and its waters hide countless thousands of coral reefs capable of bringing a vessel to its destruction. Yet four years later the *Star* returned to the spot where she had originally piled herself up; and there, capricious to the very end, she repeated the performance—for the last time!

The idea of building a lighthouse was first thought of a very long time ago. One of the Seven Wonders of the World was the Pharos, or lighthouse, of Alexandria, built by Ptolemy II of Egypt during the third century B.C. It took the form of a white marble tower, said to have been 600 feet high, and by the light of beacons kindled behind its topmost windows, vessels were guided safely into the harbour at night. The fame of this aid to navigation was spread far and wide by the mariners of those days, with the result that for many hundreds of years the word 'pharos' was the generally accepted term for a lighthouse throughout Europe. When the Romans came to Britain they built a Pharos at Dover, and this building, which still stands in the grounds of Dover Castle, is considered to be one of the most interesting relics of Roman Britain. With a similar structure on the French coast, near Boulogne, and another near Dover, it helped to guide the Roman troopships and supply vessels across the Channel.

Strangely enough, until about 300 years ago nearly all lighthouses around the British coast were privately owned. Some were built and looked after by priests who wanted to save sailors from being shipwrecked, and an excellent example of one of these towers stands on the summit of St. Catherine's Hill, Blackgang, in the Isle of Wight. Others were run for profit by people who levied tolls on ship-owners. Of course, all this made it very easy for unscrupulous people to show false lights on dangerous stretches of coast, with the object of deliberately leading ships on to the rocks. This practice of 'wrecking' was all too common at one time, and because it was done in order to plunder the vessel's cargo, little or no effort was made to save the lives of the sailors. Sometimes in fact, those who managed to swim ashore were deliberately thrown back into the sea so that no tales could be told.

However, during the reign of Henry the Eighth, when Britain began to expand her overseas trade, it became increasingly obvious that our lighthouses would have to be placed under some sort of controlling body. A royal charter was therefore granted to a semi-religious body called the Guild of the Trinity (later known as Trinity House), which had for some time been looking after the interests of English seamen and shipping. In due course this society began to build its own lighthouses, although in doing so a great deal of opposition was encountered along certain stretches of coast. Down in Cornwall, for instance, the traditions of the wreckers were still very much alive; so that when, in 1619, it was decided to erect a lighthouse on rugged Lizard Point the builders found it almost impossible to obtain local labour for the job. In a report on the situation Sir John Killigrew wrote:

'The inhabitants nearby think they suffer by this erection. They affirm I take away God's Grace from them. Their English meaning is that now they shall receive no more benefit by shipwreck for this will prevent it. They have been so long used to reap profit by the calamities of the ruin of shipping that they claim it hereditary and heavily complain on me.'

In spite of countless difficulties, however, Trinity House went ahead with its work, and with the passing of the years privately owned lighthouses became less common. It was not until 1838, however, that an Act of Parliament was passed which gave Trinity House the power to take over the last of these privately owned lighthouses. Amazing though it may seem, until 1822 some of them had still been using the old-fashioned beacon fire, just as the Romans had done, centuries before.

All Britain's very early lighthouses were situated on the shore, but in 1696 a man called Henry Winstanley built one on a lonely rock called the Eddystone, nine miles off the

131

Cornish coast, and fourteen miles S.S.W. of Plymouth Sound. It was a strange wooden contraption, perched on top of a stone base, and looked more like a Chinese pagoda than a lighthouse. It even boasted a picturesque bow window, so that the keeper of the light could catch fish while lying in bed! Seven years later this fantastic structure was washed away in a great storm, and Henry Winstanley, who was in it at the time, was drowned.

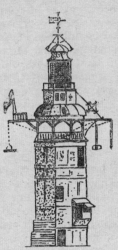

Eddystone Lighthouse
1696

The second Eddystone Lighthouse was built in 1706. It also was constructed largely of wood, and in 1755 it caught fire and was destroyed. The next lighthouse was built four years later out of huge blocks of Portland stone encased in granite. These were dove-tailed together, and the foundations dove-tailed into the rock itself. The tower was round and tapered towards the top, and it is said that John Smeaton, its designer, decided upon this shape after studying the trunk of the oak tree, which stands up so well to the strongest gales.

This principle is still used in the construction of modern lighthouses.

Until Smeaton's day open braziers filled with blazing coal and wood had provided the necessary illumination, and the task of looking after these beacons must have entailed a great deal of hard work. In his new lighthouse, however, Smeaton decided to use tallow candles, burning two dozen at a time in

Eddystone Lighthouse
1706

a large chandelier. Compare this with the lantern of the modern Eddystone light, which has a brilliancy that is equal to 358,000 candles!

John Smeaton's lighthouse stood on the Eddystone for over 120 years, but in the end the rock on which it had been built become undermined by the sea, and a new lighthouse had to be constructed on a fresh site nearby. The old lighthouse was then taken down stone by stone and ferried across to the mainland. It was rebuilt on Plymouth Hoe as a monument, and people visiting the town today are allowed to climb up inside it to the top. Fourteen miles away the new Eddystone lighthouse may be seen, poking up out of the sea.

Beside it, on an adjacent rock, is the base of Smeaton's lighthouse, standing above the waves like the stump of a felled tree.

Although lighthouses built on the shore are more numerous than those situated far out to sea, it is the latter type,

Eddystone Lighthouse
1759

remote and wave-lashed, which fire the public's imagination. Many people must have wondered what life is like for the men who spend months on end perched above the surging waters in one of these offshore lighthouses. As a matter of fact their duties are so varied that time does not hang so heavily on their hands as many people might suppose. The lantern and fog siren have to be serviced during the daytime; a continuous watch must be maintained on passing shipping and the weather; regular radio contact has to be maintained with the shore; there is the log book to be written up, stores to be checked, meals prepared, and any number of other domestic chores requiring constant attention.

Many offshore lighthouse keepers take a keen interest in

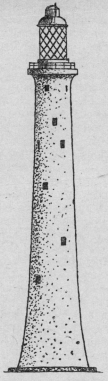

Eddystone Lighthouse
1882

the habits of the sea birds; creatures for which they must feel a certain affinity. Another favourite pastime is fishing; although wind, height, and the surrounding rocks usually combine to make ordinary rod and line angling impossible. Instead, the men have to resort to some very unusual methods. For instance, on Wolf Rock, which lies eight miles off Land's End, they spend many pleasant hours fishing by kite. A baited hook and line is attached to the tail of the

135

kite; whilst a trip line gives it a 'bit of bias'—to quote the expression used by the lighthouse men. This is necessary so that the baited hook may be whipped up and down in the water, plumbing various depths, and striking the hook home when a fish takes the bait.

Sometimes this skill at kite flying proves useful for other purposes, as was the case just before Christmas, 1952. The keepers of Wolf Rock Lighthouse should have been relieved early in December, but continuous rough seas had kept them marooned, despite repeated attempts by the Trinity House tender *Satellite* to get them home for Christmas. On Christmas Eve conditions were as bad as ever, but Captain C. F. Horn, master of the *Satellite*, sent off the vessel's motor launch with a few seasonal luxuries.

The kite was launched from a window about eighty feet up the side of the tower, and by skilful use of the trip line the keepers made it dive straight into the boat. To the tail of the kite the boat's crew tied a package of Christmas mail, and with the assistance of the wind this was quickly hauled into the lighthouse. The operation was repeated many times, and the kite flew back and forth between boat and lighthouse with tins containing the all-important Christmas dinner dangling from its tail.

Being marooned in a lighthouse is no joke at any time, but should one of the keepers fall seriously ill during a period of severe storms the situation can become critical. A comparatively minor illness like appendicitis can prove fatal if surgical treatment is not forthcoming promptly, and often at such times the sea seems to take a fiendish delight in pitting its strength against the skilled crews of the Trinity House relief vessels. As I write I have before me a paragraph torn from my daily paper. It reads as follows: 'For the second day running rough seas yesterday prevented a lighthouse ship taking off a keeper who is seriously ill in Sule Skerry Lighthouse, thirty miles west of the Orkneys.' To many readers those few words might not have seemed very interesting or exciting; yet high drama, and sometimes tragedy, lies behind a brief newspaper statement like that.

Strange things have happened from time to time in the

lonely, wave-lashed beacons which guard the seaways of Britain. To this day, for instance, there are some who still discuss the mysterious events which occurred over half a century ago in the Eilean Mor Lighthouse. This remote tower derives its name from the largest of the uninhabited Flannan Islands, on which it stands far out in the Atlantic, seventeen miles west of the Island of Lewis.

Eilean Mor Lighthouse was completed in December, 1899, and for twelve months the 140,000 candle-power lantern sent its beam swinging out across the restless ocean. Then, on the night of December 15th, 1900, the light failed to appear. People on the Island of Lewis who noticed its absence were at a loss to find an explanation; for three men were manning Eilean Mor at the time, and it seemed scarcely possible that all were so incapacitated by illness that none could attend to the lantern. Unfortunately, a storm blew up on the following day, and it was not until Boxing Day, eleven days later, that the lighthouse tender *Hesperus* was able to visit Eilean Mor to investigate the mystery.

For mystery it most certainly proved to be. When those aboard the *Hesperus* landed on the rugged little island they found no trace of the lighthouse keepers. Three men, experienced, reliable, and wise in the ways of the sea, had vanished completely, as though into thin air. Nor were they ever seen or heard of again.

· · · · ·

Since Smeaton's chandelier of twenty-four candles glimmered out across the Channel for the first time there have been many improvements in the methods of lighthouse illumination. Oil lamps with flat wicks came into use round about 1763. Then, about twenty years later, it was discovered that a wick in the form of a hollow cylinder gave a much brighter light, because the air was able to rise both inside and outside the flame. With the additional refinement of a glass chimney, which made for a cleaner and steadier flame, the illumination of lighthouses rapidly became more efficient. At the same time, though, it must be remembered that the cheap and clean-burning paraffin oil which we take for granted today was practically unknown until well into the nineteenth century. Consequently, the majority of these early lamp-lit lighthouses were fuelled with oil obtained from the sperm whale. Later on colza oil was used, a vegetable product extracted from the seeds of the rape plant. Nowadays, so far as offshore lighthouses are concerned, incandescent burners are in general use, and the brilliancy of the light is greatly intensified by a complicated system of lenses and prisms.

In the early days many lighthouses displayed lights of various colours, so that the mariner might distinguish one from another, and not mistake his position. This had several disadvantages, however. The number of colours which could be used was very limited, and duplication was unavoidable. Also, it was discovered that a coloured lens cut down the power of the light. A lantern shining through red glass, for example, casts a beam with less than half the power of that from a similar lantern shining through clear glass. In the same way, a green light is only a quarter as powerful as a white one. At the beginning of the nineteenth century, however, a revolving light was placed on top of Flamborough Head, in Yorkshire, and this was the forerunner of the modern flashing light, which automatically sends out its own particular recognition code at regular intervals. Some of these revolving lanterns have lenses weighing many tons, and in order that they may rotate easily they are mounted on a platform which floats in a circular trough of mercury.

It is, however, in connection with unattended lights that some of the cleverest inventions have been made. A delicate instrument known as a sun-valve distinguishes between night and day, automatically switching on the light at dusk, and turning it off again at daybreak. There is also a remarkable device which automatically replaces a gas mantle or electric lamp as soon as it becomes damaged. Most wonderful of all, though, is a device that has only recently been perfected by the scientific research workers of Trinity House. It is a self-acting fog siren, operated by an invisible radar beam that is constantly sent out by the lighthouse. In clear atmosphere this beam passes on into space, but when intercepted by a bank of fog it is reflected back to the lighthouse, where it automatically sets the fog-horn bellowing a warning to nearby shipping.

Although there have been instances of wave-washed lighthouses being built on sand, the absence of a firm foundation makes the operation very difficult and expensive. Therefore, a dangerous shoal of sand or mud is usually marked by a lightship—a strong, steel-built vessel between 80 and 120 feet long, and with a displacement of 200–500 tons. The first lightship was stationed at the Nore in 1732, the light

British lightship

being an ordinary storm lantern suspended from the yardarm. Today, the equipment of a lightship is very similar to that of a lighthouse, although the rolling of the vessel necessitates some modifications to the lantern in order to maintain a horizontal beam of light. This is done by a variety of devices, most of them making use of gymbals, pendulums, or counter-balance weights. Incidentally, the lantern is always referred to by the lightshipmen as the 'moon-box'.

The normal crew for a British lightship is seven men, and it is the proud boast of this section of Trinity House that they possess the finest 'sea legs' in the world. They certainly need strong stomachs; for there is nothing that puts a sailor to the test more than being at sea in an anchored ship. Lightships, of course, are anchored all the time and, being comparatively small vessels, they pitch and roll to every wave.

Few people, in fact, would envy the lightshipmen their lot during a fierce storm, when every few hours the watch-keeper on duty has to struggle up the stubby lantern mast to inspect the moon-box. Even for those off duty there can be little rest, with the rusty anchor chains grinding through the hawse-holes, filling the metal-hulled ship with an appalling din. To the ordinary sailor, being aboard a lightship in a severe gale would be a terrifying experience, for the vessel has neither engine nor sails, and only the anchors—which are shaped like huge mushrooms—stand between uncomfortable safety and complete disaster. There can be no running for harbour if things get too bad. One can only hang on to the ship as it plunges and wallows, and try to forget the indisputable fact that an anchor chain is only as strong as its weakest link.

Sometimes disaster does come to a lightship. In 1953 the crew of the St. Gowan's Lightship, ten miles off the Pembrokeshire coast, had to be rescued by the Tenby Lifeboat during a terrific gale. The lightship had been swamped by huge seas, the pumps were out of action, and the vessel had taken on a list of forty-five degrees. The mechanism which operated the revolving lantern had also failed; yet, though the lightship was in imminent danger of capsizing, the crew took it in turns to clamber up the swaying thirty-foot mast to turn the lantern by hand. Not until the lifeboat appeared three hours before dawn, in answer to their S O S, did they leave the lantern and abandon ship.

In a severe gale a lightship tends to sit back on her cable, as though trying to weigh anchor all by herself, and the crew have to keep a watchful eye on their mooring. One of the most exposed lightships around our coasts is the *Seven Stones,* stationed out in the Atlantic between the Scilly Isles and the Cornish mainland. In heavy seas this vessel has to be allowed plenty of scope—that is to say a lot more cable has to be paid out in order to prevent her from dragging her anchor. There have been times when, in the face of a wild sou'wester, the hands aboard have been compelled to reel

140

out well over a third of a mile of chain. On such occasions, no doubt, the crew find great consolation from the knowledge that every single link in those chains has been hand-forged by master craftsmen, and afterwards tested again and again for any possible signs of weakness.

Even so, there have been times when, in spite of careful nursing on the part of the crew, the anchors of a lightship have been unable to withstand the really exceptional strains to which they are occasionally subjected. For a whole week in February, 1936, the coasts of Britain were blasted by a south-east gale of hurricane force, and on the fourth day a message was received at the Ballycotton Lifeboat Station, in Ireland, to the effect that the Daunt Rock Lightship was adrift from her moorings, and was being carried towards the shore. The lifeboat put out to sea at once, and after some searching found that the lightship had fetched up very close to the Daunt Rock, and was being hurled about by mountainous seas. A British destroyer was standing by, and attempts were made to tow the helpless vessel clear, but so great was the force of the wind that the stout hawsers snapped like pieces of string. Later on the wind moderated a little, and the destroyer resumed her voyage when it was learned that a towing vessel was proceeding to the scene from Dublin. The wind sprang up again shortly afterwards, however, and soon the seas were worse than ever. One huge wave swept right over the lightship, carrying away one of the two red lights which are shown by a lightship when she is not at her station. It then became obvious to Coxswain Pat Sliney of the lifeboat that neither the lightship nor its crew could take much more punishment, and he decided to try to take the men off the stricken vessel. The lightship's violently swinging anchor chains made coming alongside a very dangerous operation, but by reversing again and again under the vessel's plunging stern the Coxswain managed to rescue all the lightship's crew, one at a time. All told, the rescue operations took sixty-three hours, and when the lifeboat returned to Ballycotton it had been away from its station for over seventy six hours.

Another danger which the crews of the lightships have to

141

face is the risk of being run down in thick fog by some large ocean-going vessel. This was the fate of the old Gull Lightship, and Trinity House men talk of the tragedy to this day. From out of a world of writhing white vapour there suddenly appeared the huge wedge of steel-plated bows, and the tiny lightship was cut almost in two. The Master was drowned in his cabin; and within a matter of seconds the vessel was sinking beneath the crew as they worked frantically to lower the only undamaged lifeboat.

However, with the advent of the Second World War, all these normal perils of the sea were overshadowed by far greater dangers. The inoffensive lightships, helpful to friend and foe alike, were subjected to incessant attacks by enemy aircraft, and the men aboard found themselves face to face with Eternity time and time again. Unarmed, and unable to manœuvre, they were compelled to remain on their ships and accept whatever the German Luftwaffe chose to hand out. Especially hard-hit were the lightships around the Thames Estuary, and one after another these gallant little vessels—some of them wooden and nearly a century old—were sent to the bottom by bombs, mines and cannon fire. The first to be attacked was the Smith's Knoll lightship, on 11th January, 1940. After that the assaults grew steadily more frequent, until eventually they totalled well over a hundred.

So there you have a picture of the lighthouses and lightships in peace and war—and of the men who tend them. The life of a light-keeper is a hard one: lonely, uncomfortable, and sometimes dangerous. Yet, in spite of the hardships, these men derive a certain satisfaction from their calling; for the sea is in their blood, and they are seamen in every sense of the word. Hard-bitten some of them may be, but they are men of honour, with an extremely high sense of duty. Industrial workers on shore may have their 'sit-down strikes', or 'work to rule', but these men of Trinity House know that theirs is a job of mercy—and, come what may, they see to it that the lights keep shining out across the dark and treacherous waters.

Two hundred years ago the unfortunate sailor whose ship was wrecked in stormy seas was almost certain to drown. Even when disaster occurred close to the land there was little hope. The people on shore could only watch with feelings of bitter impotence as the crew of the foundered vessel were swept overboard one by one into the thundering breakers. The lifeboat had yet to be invented.

Englishmen have a right to be proud of the fact that the construction and operation of the world's first lifeboat sprang from the compassion, foresight, skill and courage of a number of their countrymen. In 1785 a London coachbuilder called Lionel Lukin got the idea of making a boat that would not sink, even though it might become completely filled with water. Although a landsman, his methods were sound ; due, perhaps, to the fact that he was descended from one of Admiral's Blake's captains. He bought a Norway yawl and fitted her with numerous air-filled buoyancy chambers, projecting cork gunwales, and a heavy iron keel. The air boxes made the vessel unsinkable ; while the cork gunwales and heavy keel were intended to lessen the risk of capsizing.

The result was an extremely seaworthy craft, which Lukin put into the hands of an experienced seaman for extensive rough-weather trials. The yawl repeatedly crossed the Channel when all other boats were storm-bound in harbour, but unfortunately the seaman whom Lukin had appointed as skipper of the craft began to use her for carrying contraband liquor, and she was seized by the Customs and broken up. Nevertheless, she had proved her worth, and Lukin at once set to work on building another boat on similar lines. His object, however, was not to construct a lifeboat, but to perfect a method of making all sea-going vessels so safe that lifeboats would be unnecessary.

Lukin patented his 'unimmergible boat', as he termed his invention, and in 1786 received a coble from a clergyman called Archdeacon Sharp, who was the Vicar of Bamburgh, on the Northumberland coast. Appalled by the number of shipwrecks which had occurred along the shores of his parish, the clergyman wished to have this local form of fishing craft turned into a lifeboat. Lukin applied his 'unimmergible' principles to the boat, and in the same year it was installed at Bamburgh as the world's first shore-based lifeboat.

For a while the fine example set by Lionel Lukin and Archdeacon Sharp had little effect upon the general public. But the fishermen of Bamburgh who manned the lifeboat were soon proving that saving life from a shipwreck was possible with the right type of equipment, and it was inevitable that, sooner or later, this fact should stir the consciences of others. In 1789 the terrible wreck of the *Adventure* occurred off the mouth of the Tyne with the loss of many lives, and a number of influential men of South Shields, who witnessed the disaster, decided to do their utmost to prevent such a thing happening again. First of all, therefore, they offered a prize of two guineas to anyone who submitted a plan or model of a lifeboat suitable for use off the mouth of the Tyne during a severe storm.

A number of people responded to the offer, but the most revolutionary idea came from a local house-painter called William Wouldhave—a public-spirited individual who, in his spare time, taught singing to charity children and performed the duties of parish clerk. Wouldhave submitted a model of an unsinkable boat which automatically righted itself when capsized.

The idea of making this self-righting lifeboat came to him in a rather unusual way. One day, while walking along a country lane, he came upon a woman who had just drawn a bucket of water from a well. Wouldhave noticed that the bucket was too heavy for the woman, so he offered to help carrying it to her nearby cottage. The woman gratefully accepted his offer, and the house-painter stooped to pick up the bucket. As he did so he noticed half a wooden bowl floating on top of the water, like a tiny boat. Forgetting all about the woman, Wouldhave began absent-mindedly playing with this piece of wood. To his surprise, whenever he turned the broken bowl upside-down in the water it immediately righted itself, and his native wit at once told him that here was an idea which could be applied to a lifeboat. He made a model boat on somewhat similar lines to the fragment of wooden bowl and submitted it to the committee that had offered the prize of two guineas.

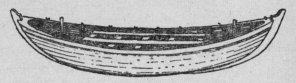

An early lifeboat drawn from the model made by
Henry Greathead
(NOTE: The cork fenders are not shown)

William Wouldhave's model earned for him a half-share of the reward. Some of his ideas were then combined with those of several other people, and another model was constructed out of clay for the guidance of a South Shields boat-builder who had been commissioned to make the actual lifeboat. Henry Greathead was the name of this craftsman, and there can be little doubt that he put a great deal of thought and skill into the job entrusted to him. When completed, his boat measured 30 feet from stem to stern, with a 10-foot beam, and a depth of 3 feet 3 inches amidships. Along either side there stretched a massive cork fender, whilst buoyancy was further increased by two cork linings, running fore and aft along the inside of the craft.

This lifeboat, which was named the *Original*, was launched in January, 1790. It had cost £76 9s. 8d.—a very considerable sum for those days. She soon proved her worth, however, for she made her first life-saving mission only a few days later, and during her forty years of service she made countless others.

145

The success of the *Original* brought Henry Greathead orders for similar lifeboats from many parts of the country, and even from abroad. All told, he built thirty-one lifeboats; eighteen for service in England, five for Scotland, and eight for use abroad. In addition, he received considerable financial recognition. Parliament made him a grant of £1,200; the Society of Arts presented him with a gold medal and fifty guineas; whilst Trinity House and Lloyd's insurance brokers made him a gift of 100 guineas. Lloyd's also gave £2,000 towards the cost of Greathead's lifeboats; thus beginning a tradition which continues to this day—for Lloyd's have always contributed generously to the funds of the Royal National Lifeboat Institution.

Meanwhile, Lionel Lukin was still working on his 'unimmergible boat', although without the same heartening amount of recognition. In 1807, however, he received an order for a lifeboat from the Suffolk Humane Society, and this proved so successful that it became the forerunner of the extremely seaworthy 'Norfolk' and 'Suffolk' type of lifeboat. Lukin designed his lifeboats for sailing as well as rowing; whereas Greathead's boats were propelled by oars alone.

Although a number of lifeboats were now installed around our shores, manned by fishermen who knew every inch of the coast they guarded, it could not truthfully be said that we possessed a really efficient lifeboat service. This was no fault of the crews, who time after time performed miracles of courage and seamanship. The fault lay in the organisation—or, rather, the lack of it. There was a crying need for some sort of centralised body, which could concentrate on the improvement of life-saving equipment and rescue methods, whilst at the same time looking after the financial interests of the lifeboatmen.

For this reason the idea of forming the Royal National Lifeboat Institution was conceived by Lieutenant-Colonel Sir William Hillary. Although a soldier, he appears to have always been interested in maritime matters, for it is recorded that he used to sail an open boat for pleasure, when such a pastime was almost unheard of amongst members of the 'gentry'.

146

For many years Sir William lived at Douglas, on the Isle of Man, and it was during this period that a series of dreadful shipwrecks occurred in Douglas Bay. In one winter alone no less than twelve vessels were lost, including two naval ships, the *Racehorse* and the *Vigilant*. The island possessed no lifeboat, but the local fishermen, with Sir William Hillary amongst them, courted death a hundred times by going out to the rescue in small boats which had never been designed to survive a storm. Two hundred and thirty-eight lives were saved from these twelve wrecks, and in every rescue Sir William was an outstanding figure.

Reckless of his own safety though he was, Sir William Hillary realised only too well that it was wrong for the country to expect the fishermen to continue risking their lives indefinitely without providing them with proper equipment. He therefore drafted a plan for a properly organised, country-wide lifeboat service, which he published in 1823 under the title *An Appeal to the British Nation*. In his plan he proposed that lifeboat crews should consist of volunteers who were to be rewarded whenever they made a rescue attempt. Also, the dependants of a lifeboatman who lost his life whilst on service were to be assured of a pension. These matters, and the stationing of really efficient lifeboats all round the British coast, were to be the responsibility of the entire British nation, and all classes of people were to be invited to contribute voluntarily to the scheme.

The appeal bore fruit, and the following year a public meeting was held in London, which resulted in the foundation of the Royal National Lifeboat Institution. Sir William Hillary's proposals were adopted, and to this day they remain unchanged in all important respects. Every part-time member of a lifeboat crew is still a volunteer, and he is under no obligation to put out in the lifeboat when the alarm is given. Yet, no matter how bad the weather conditions may be, men always answer the call; far more, in fact, than are actually required.

As we have already seen, Sir William Hillary was essentially a man of action, and he was not content to be a mere figurehead of the Institution. He was not happy until he had

147

acquired four badly needed lifeboats for the Isle of Man, and had volunteered to help crew the one stationed at Douglas. This particular boat was installed in November, 1830, and hardly had it been delivered before a terrific gale blew up in the bay. The Royal Mail steamer *St. George*, which was lying some distance offshore, lost her anchors at the height of the storm, and in a matter of minutes had been driven on to the rocks. There had been no time as yet to equip the new lifeboat properly, and the local fishermen were of the opinion that she was unfit to launch in such a raging sea. Sir William Hillary, however, managed to persuade sixteen of them to put out with him, and after a tremendous struggle they managed to rescue the steamer's entire crew of twenty-two. Nevertheless, the trip nearly cost Sir William his life, for a huge sea washed him and three other members of the lifeboat's crew overboard. The others managed to save them, but the accident had crushed Hillary's chest and broken six of his ribs. No sooner had he been hauled back into the boat, however, than he resumed his duties.

At the time of the *St. George* rescue Sir William Hillary was fifty-nine years of age, and it would not have been surprising if his injuries had caused him to retire for good from his place in the lifeboat's crew. Yet we read of him going out to other wrecks, and distinguishing himself at the age of sixty-four, when he and his men rescued fifty-four people from the *Parkfield,* of Liverpool. When eventually he died at the age of seventy-eight he had played a leading part in the saving of 305 lives, and had three times won the R.N.L.I. Gold Medal for outstanding gallantry. No wonder that Sir William Hillary is still remembered as one of the greatest lifeboatmen ever.

From its inception the R.N.L.I. strove continually to improve its lifeboats and their equipment, although for many years the work of the Institution in this direction was greatly hampered by financial difficulties. In addition, information concerning the rescue methods used by various lifeboat crews was pooled and redistributed, so that the lifeboatmen on one part of the coast might learn from the experiences of their comrades elsewhere. In such a dangerous calling as theirs it was inevitable that accidents should occur sometimes, but the details of these misfortunes were carefully studied by R.N.L.I. officials in an endeavour to prevent similar disasters from occurring again.

Although William Wouldhave had invented the principle of the self-righting lifeboat in 1789, his idea was shelved for many years, despite a number of tragedies caused through lifeboats capsizing. Many of these accidents occurred during the extremely dangerous operation of launching and beaching, and it is doubtful whether under such circumstances the self-righting principle would have been of much use. But in 1843 an accident befell a Yorkshire lifeboat which might have had a happier ending had it been built as a 'self-righter'. The *Ann*, of London, ran aground in Robin Hood's Bay; and the local lifeboat went to her assistance. When the lifeboat drew alongside the wreck, five of the *Ann*'s crew jumped down into it at the same time, just as the lifeboat was struck by a beam sea. The force of the wave, coupled with the sudden additional weight of the five men, capsized the boat. Three members of the lifeboat's crew survived to give their account of the disaster, and they owed their lives to the fact that they were trapped in a pocket of air beneath the boat, and were thus able to breathe until the boat fetched up on the beach.

Six years later another lifeboat overturned, and twenty out of her crew of twenty-four men were drowned. Ironically enough, this ill-fated craft was the *Providence*, of South Shields, and the disaster occurred within sight of William Wouldhave's home town. As the bodies were pulled from the sea, many of those on the beach must have thought of the local house-painter who, sixty years before, had thought of a way of making a self-righting lifeboat. And all must have regretted bitterly the fact that his advice had not been taken.

The sacrifice made by those gallant men of South Shields was not entirely in vain, however; for the loss made a large section of the public realise at last just how much they owed to the lifeboatmen of Britain. Contributions to the Institution increased in size and number, and the possibilities of the self-righting lifeboat were once again explored. When the Duke of Northumberland became President of the R.N.L.I. in 1851 he offered a reward of 100 guineas to the person who submitted the best model of a lifeboat. There was a great response to his offer, and the prize eventually went to James Beeching, who lived at Great Yarmouth. His lifeboat incorporated the self-righting principle, much as Wouldhave had originally conceived it. Huge air-cases, or 'end-boxes', as they were called, were set high at the bows and stern, and these had sufficient buoyancy to support the entire weight of the craft if she happened to capsize. But it was virtually impossible for the lifeboat to float in that position for long because a heavy iron keel made her extremely unstable, and within a matter of seconds she would roll over again and float the right way up.

James Beeching's boat was built in considerable numbers, but before long many lifeboat crews were beginning to distrust it. They declared that the high end-boxes caught the wind, making this type of boat extremely difficult to handle in rough weather. Apart from this, it was also found that the self-righting lifeboat was, in fact, much more liable to capsize than the ordinary type, which was not designed to right itself. The R.N.L.I., always anxious to supply the type of lifeboat in which the crews had most confidence, decided in 1887 to abandon the self-righting principle so far as its large sailing lifeboats were concerned. After the turn of the century this policy was extended to cover the larger motor-driven boats, so that today only a very small proportion of self-righting lifeboats are still in service.

The first power-driven lifeboat was the *Duke of Northumberland*, a fifty-foot steam vessel stationed at Harwich. Strangely enough, she was jet-propelled—her engines pumping in great quantities of water through the bottom of the boat, and then discharging it again under tremendous pressure through underwater jets at the sides. At full speed the *Duke of Northumberland* travelled at nine knots, and took in and ejected a ton of water every second!

Some may wonder why the R.N.L.I. should have chosen such an unusual method of propulsion for their first power lifeboat. The reason was that its designers feared that an ordinary marine propeller might become entangled with the trailing ropes which often surround a wrecked sailing vessel. In all, six steam lifeboats were built, some jet-propelled and some screw-driven, but after extensive trials they proved too heavy for general service.

It was not until a reliable internal combustion engine became available that the power-driven lifeboat became

Modern motor lifeboat

popular. These craft, by crashing their way through heavy seas at a speed of eight or nine knots, are today able to save lives which would undoubtedly have been lost in the days of the old pulling and sailing lifeboats.

The modern motor lifeboat is a miracle of engineering, and is the result of continuous mechanical reseach dating from 1904. The engine is completely watertight, and will run and lubricate itself with the engine-room flooded, or while the boat is standing on end. Yet, should the lifeboat happen to capsize, the engine will stop automatically, so that there is no risk of the crew being left floating in the water while their craft goes on without them. The modern lifeboat is also fitted with a system of non-return valves, so that immediately any water comes aboard it is discharged into the sea again. As an additional safeguard there are motor-driven pumps, powerful enough to keep the boat afloat even it if becomes badly holed below the waterline.

The equipment of the present-day lifeboat also includes numerous life-saving devices, such as oil-sprays for making less rough the surface of the sea in the vicinity of a wreck; a searchlight for illuminating rescue operations; a line-throwing gun or pistol; a loud hailer, and a radio transmitting and receiving set. In the most recent types of lifeboat the loud hailer is worked in conjunction with the radio, so that at the mere flick of a switch the radio operator can contact either his shore station, or the crew of a wrecked vessel. This can be a most valuable time-saver in a situation where every second counts.

The years between the First and Second World Wars saw the main change-over of the Lifeboat Service from sail to motor-driven craft. Many readers, however, may be surprised to learn that the last sailing lifeboat remained in commission until December, 1948. Because of the unavoidable risks of explosion associated with the use of a petrol engine in an enclosed boat, the R.N.L.I. now favours diesel power for its lifeboats. In fact, there is a steady change-over now in progress from the old single-engined craft to a fleet of more powerful and reliable boats, all equipped with two engines and twin screws.

Thus the Institution maintains its policy of providing its lifeboat crews with nothing but the very best craft and equipment. It is, of course, an expensive policy. A modern lifeboat costs as much as £20,000; whilst the building in which it is housed, and the launching slip, may cost even more. The majority of these lifeboat houses are open to the public during the holiday season, and the visitor cannot help but be impressed by the obvious care with which the craft are maintained. The gleaming brasswork, the beautiful sheer of the glistening blue, red and white hull, will delight the eye of anyone, whether they be seafarer or landlubber.

When we remember that the R.N.L.I. has stationed 155 of these lifeboats around the coasts of the United Kingdom, Eire, and the Channel Islands—all costing tens of thousands of pounds, and all maintained at the same high degree of efficiency—we begin to realise what a wonderful thing is this life-saving service. We feel proud, and rightly so. The

Royal National Lifeboat Institution, built up with British courage and craftsmanship, was setting an example to the rest of the world nearly a century and a half ago, and it continues to do so today.

The cost of maintaining and renewing the lifeboats and their equipment amounts to some £750,000 every year, and it is worth remembering that all this money comes from voluntary contributions made by the men, women and children of this country. That is one of the reasons why the lifeboat stations are open to visitors. The Royal National Lifeboat Institution likes the public to see how its money is being spent; and the public, when they have seen for themselves, are more than satisfied. In every lifeboat house notice-boards are displayed which give details of the services rendered over the years by the lifeboats of that particular station. Many of these brief log entries could be expanded into thrilling sagas of the sea, and the figures recording the number of lives saved in each instance make impressive reading. Since its foundation, in fact, the Institution has saved the lives of more than 86,591 people, with a present-day average of 750 lives saved every year. Truly, this is a remarkable achievement. As we end this short account of the growth of our modern Lifeboat Service, let us try to imagine the difficulties which had to be encountered and overcome, the dangers which had to be braved and beaten, to accomplish such a wonderful record.

For the majority of people who live by the sea all the year round, beachcombing is little more than an excuse to go for a tramp along the shore on a winter afternoon. It is true that on haphazard expeditions of this sort the amateur beach-comber does occasionally find something really useful, but more often than not he—or she—returns home with nothing more exciting than a bundle of firewood.

Yet beachcombing can be worth while if one sets about it in the right way, and during the past 20 years our own stretch of coast has presented us with quite a number of useful finds, including several gold rings, over a hundred-weight of lead fishing weights, revolver bullets and old musket balls; an ancient dagger and Roman coins (unearthed by cliff falls); about half a dozen ladders, a crate of canned Australian beer; a waterproof canister of tea; a football; a nylon parachute, a child's rocking horse; a tinned chicken; a shove-ha'penny board; dozens of ship's brooms, dan buoys and lengths of rope—to mention just a few items which come to mind.

There is, in fact, no telling what the tide will bring in next, and several rather startling things have been deposited on our local shores, among them being a German torpedo, a landmine, a capsized boat, the headless body of a man, two escaped Borstal boys, and a woman's leg, still clad in a silk stocking.

Although winter is generally regarded as being the beach-combing season proper, the summer months present plenty of opportunities as well. Summer storms are rarely severe, but they are more apt to take people by surprise than those of winter, so that more things get washed out to sea—and washed in again farther along the coast. I know of one early-rising longshoreman who came upon no less than half a dozen deck-chairs and a beach tent after a stiff mid-August sou'-wester; thus proving once again the advantage of 'getting there before the other fellow'. Small objects may evade dozens of questing eyes, and eventually be picked up by a late-comer, but for all that it is best to be down on the beach after a storm just as soon as the first high tide is on the turn.

It should be borne in mind, though, that quite often the best hauls are made several days after a storm has passed away, when the sea has calmed down again. This is because it takes some time for goods washed overboard from ships far out at sea to drift ashore. On certain stretches of coast, especially around rocky headlands, there are places where, owing to the set of the currents, more stuff is washed ashore than elsewhere. It is up to the novice at beachcombing to make a mental note of these places as they are discovered, and to observe how their yields vary according to the wind direction during each storm.

Most beachcombers, both amateur and professional, cherish at the back of their mind the fond hope that they may some day chance upon a lump of stranded ambergris— floating gold, many call it. This 'grey amber' is a fatty substance excreted by the sperm or cachalot whale, and as it is very buoyant there is always a chance that some may find its way to British shores; although the creatures which produce it do not frequent our waters. It has a musky smell when warmed, and is greatly esteemed by perfume manufacturers as a fixative for more pleasant scents, with the result that extremely high prices are paid for it. There is also a ready demand for ambergris as a medicine in catarrhal infections and nervous diseases.

Personally, I have never found any ambergris, although one day while beachcombing near Girvan, on the Ayrshire coast, I did realise a boyhood ambition by discovering a message in a bottle. Visions of a bearded shipwrecked mariner, existing precariously on some far-distant desert island, rose before me as I extracted a neat little cylinder of paper from the neck of the bottle. Closer inspection, however, revealed that my find consisted merely of a bundle of tracts denouncing the evils of strong drink. According to a covering letter they had been cast into the sea exactly a fortnight before, from some place in Northern Ireland. Oddly enough, the bottle that had borne this teetotal literature across the sea emitted a strong aroma of Irish whiskey!

So far, true to longshore custom, we have tended to ignore the legal aspect of beachcombing. The fact has to be faced, however, that around the shores of Britain anything in the nature of wreckage, or cargo from a wrecked vessel, should be reported to the local receiver of wrecks. This procedure is laid down in the Merchant Shipping Act of 1894, which also states that the wreck shall remain in the keeping of the receiver for one year. After that time, if no one has established a claim to possession, the goods become the property of the Crown.

The law of wreck would therefore appear to discourage beachcombing, but it is doubtful whether it does. Naturally enough, receivers of wreck have no desire to be bothered with trifling finds, and as a rule beachcombers are left to take home their spoils, or report them, as conscience or sense of discretion dictates. On our own stretch of coast, for instance, there is a general belief that, so far as timber is concerned, pieces under eight feet long are the finder's property, whilst boards over that length may be claimed by the local receiver. Just what the foundation for this 'ruling' is I have never been able to discover; and, although often quoted amongst the beachcombing fraternity, it does not seem to have much effect. It is no unusual thing to see a stalwart gum-booted figure staggering homewards with a baulk of timber over his shoulder fully twenty feet long.

Perhaps, therefore, the popular viewpoint of the legal ins and outs of beachcombing may best be summed up by quoting, not the Merchant Shipping Act, but an old longshoreman acquaintance of mine. 'Beachcombin'?' this old rascal has been known to declare. 'Why, that'm like poachin', zee you. 'Tis a-gettin' zomething' f'r nuthen—but it bain't stealin'!'

Ever since the day when, as a small boy, I read Robert Louis Stevenson's *Treasure Island,* I have been filled with a sneaking desire to discover an item of treasure trove of my own.

Fanciful, you say? Far-fetched? Not at all! You don't have to charter a vessel and sail away to the South Seas in order to hunt for your 'pieces of eight'. Vast quantities of treasure lie hidden in every part of Britain, and it is no exaggeration to say that many of you who read this book will already have walked unwittingly within a few yards of some buried hoard.

Although it is a subject that must have captured the imagination of most people at one time or another, it is surprising how few really know the law of treasure trove. Briefly, treasure trove may be defined as gold or silver of unknown ownership found hidden in the earth or elsewhere. According to Roman law it belonged to the finder if found on his own land. If found on someone else's land, half went to the finder and half to the landowner. In modern English law, however, wherever found it belongs to the Crown, and to conceal it is punishable by fine or imprisonment. But in 1886 the Home Office decided to allow finders to keep anything not wanted for a museum or similar national institution; whilst any article retained for a museum would be paid for at its full antiquarian value.

This island of ours has enjoyed a pretty chequered history, and during its course there have been many good reasons why its inhabitants should secrete their valuables. The uncertainty of life and absence of safe banking facilities at the time of the Civil War must have been one of the main causes; whilst the dissolution of the monasteries brought about the disappearance underground of large quantities of church plate.

These two reasons for the concealment of valuables apply equally to places situated inland and on the coast. Yet it is a fact that there is a much better chance of finding treasure on or near the coasts of Britain than inland. There are several reasons for this. In very early times, when our coasts were frequently harried by sea raiders, the inhabitants of our shores very wisely kept their valuables well hidden so that they could make themselves scarce at a second's notice when an attack was imminent. Sometimes, however, it happened that an entire community would be taken completely by surprise and butchered, and then the wealth that had been hidden so cunningly would remain forgotten and neglected through the long centuries.

Similarly, in later times, pirates and wreckers frequently found difficulty in disposing of their spoils, and would hide them away near the coast until a suitable market presented itself. The buccaneers especially led a precarious existence; entire crews were shipwrecked and drowned, or were captured and hanged for their crimes at Execution Dock. Since dead men can tell no tales, their hidden booty became lost to the world—until chance chose to reveal it to some lucky person, perhaps hundreds of years later.

Seaside treasure trove has come to light in some strange ways. To this day the glint of gold is to be seen on our beaches after a combination of high spring tide and stormy sea have turned over countless millions of tons of pebbles. Cliff falls and other forms of coast erosion also reveal some startling treasures. Workmen excavating the foundations for a sea wall have been known to strike it rich, filling their pockets in a few minutes with golden guineas. But perhaps the most surprising find of all was when some children, playing 'treasure-hunters' among some lonely sand dunes, actually unearthed a pirate hoard of gold, silver and precious gems with their wooden spades.

Not all treasure is found by pure chance, though. There have been instances of untold riches coming the way of people who, on hearing some local legend about a hidden hoard, have been astute enough to realise that there might be a grain of truth in what everyone else had come to regard as a mere 'old wives' tale'.

Such a case occurred some years ago at a small fishing village on the west coast of Ireland. A professional diver, on a brief visit to the district, began chatting one day to a group of local fishermen about some of his experiences on the bed of the sea. After listening to him attentively for some time, one grizzled old salt suddenly made a strange remark.

'Indeed, it must be a wonderful thing to be able to walk about underneath the ocean,' he commented, wistfully. 'If I could do a thing like that I'd be after making meself a rich man, so I would.'

The diver asked the old fellow what he meant.

'Why, out in the bay there's an old Spanish galleon that went down in a great storm hundreds of years ago. Full of treasure, she was.'

The other fishermen laughed heartily. They had often heard the story of the wrecked treasure ship; so often, in fact, that it had become associated in their minds with other local tales of fairies, mermaids, and the giants of olden times.

The old fisherman, however, shook his head gravely at the scoffers. 'Treasure there is, for sure,' he persisted. 'I heard the tale from me grandfather, and he was after hearing it from his father's father. And even then the story was old. Now I ask ye—would the tale have lived as long as that if it had been but a lie?'

The diver was intrigued and impressed, and after some thought he decided to investigate the matter. He enrolled the old fisherman as his partner, and for weeks they rowed back and forth across the bay in a small boat, trailing a grappling iron behind them.

A month passed, and then one day the grappling iron caught upon some obstruction on the sea bed. The diver donned his suit and went down to investigate. Sure enough, it was the galleon—or, at any rate, what was left of her. Rotting, worm-eaten timbers poked up out of the ooze, festooned with weed and haunted by fish. But in the midst of all this decay the diver made a thrilling find. Groping around on the sea bed, he came upon what at first he took to be several small wooden barrels. Closer inspection, however, proved them to be piles of golden doubloons, each pile cemented into a solid mass by a covering of marine growths. Originally, the coins had been stored in casks; but the wooden staves had long since rotted away, leaving the gold, still retaining the shape of the casks, to become the home of seaweeds and shellfish.

There is something about a tale of hidden treasure that acts as a challenge, and makes it almost impossible to dismiss from one's mind. This fact is well illustrated by the many attempts which have been made to raise the £300,000 in golden doubloons which some say lies at the bottom of Tobermory Bay, on the north-east side of the Isle of Mull. For here, within a mile or so of the Scottish mainland, a Spanish treasure ship of the 'Invincible' Armada is reputed to have foundered in 1588. The story goes that this proud galleon put into the bay to take shelter from a storm, and whilst riding at her anchor was destroyed by a terrific explosion in her powder magazine. One version of the story tells us that the explosion was deliberately caused by a Highland chieftain, who had been captured by the Spaniards in a raid ashore. This brave man had preferred to blow himself up with the ship rather than face the humiliation of defeat, and the misery of exile and imprisonment in Spain.

This local tradition that a Spanish galleon was lost in the bay is almost certainly true, and the Duke of Argyll, who possesses the salvage rights, has spent a great deal of money on numerous treasure hunts. The wreck of an old wooden ship, buried under a thick layer of mud, has been located by several salvage parties, who also managed to bring to the surface various relics, including a collection of Spanish coins. In 1912 treasure was recovered to the value of nearly one thousand pounds. Then the First World War came to interrupt operations, and by 1919, when the task was resumed, the galleon was again buried deep in the mud. High pressure hoses were used to dig the skeleton ship out again, but during this operation the leader of the enterprise was nearly killed by a powerful jet of water, and the treasure seekers abandoned their quest.

Further attempts were made, however. The last one, which was carried out with the assistance of hired Royal Navy divers, came to an unsuccessful conclusion only a year or so previous to the writing of this book. So the treasure of Tobermory Bay, if it has ever existed, would appear to be still there, waiting for some lucky diver to dig it out of the mud.

From the west coast of Scotland let us turn our attention to the east coast of England. There is only one fact about King John that has remained in my memory since my schooldays, and that is that the unfortunate man lost his jewels in the Wash. Now there, surely, is something to challenge astute readers visiting those parts. It is only fair to mention, though, that there have always been people who openly disbelieved King John's 'lost in the Wash' story. Many declare that his treasure was, in fact, hidden in or near Rockingham Castle, where he had been staying shortly before his expensive upset off the fenland coast.

Sometimes discoveries are made which, although they do not come within the limited definition of treasure trove, nevertheless prove even more valuable than the traditional gold and precious gems. Such an instance is related in a fascinating book called *The Wonders of Salvage*, by David Masters. During the First World War a German submarine was sunk by the British in about thirty fathoms of water. The Admiralty apparently had a hunch that the submarine had been carrying some important secret documents, for they immediately issued an order to the effect that divers of their Salvage Section were to go down and investigate the wreck.

After groping their way along the hull of the submarine the divers came to the conning tower—and there a strange and gruesome sight loomed up before them in the underwater gloom. From the conning-tower hatch there stretched a human arm, clutching in its dead hand a package. Prising open the dead man's fingers, the divers took their find up to the surface. To their delight, the contents of the package proved to be the invaluable secret papers which the Admiralty were so anxious to obtain. Apparently the U-boat commander, realising that his ship was doomed, had been about to destroy his secret orders by throwing them out of the conning tower when the submarine had suddenly plunged to the bottom. The conning tower hatch had slammed shut under the pressure of the water, imprisoning his arm and paralysing his fingers, so that he was quite unable to release his grip on the papers. Thus his undeniably gallant last act was in vain. Instead of preventing his secret documents from becoming the property of the British Admiralty, he had actually offered them to us in his outstretched hand!

But let us return to more orthodox and romantic tales of treasure. For these we would be well advised to travel down to the West Country, because it is in that part of Britain that the majority of buried treasure legends are to be found. The gaunt, hill-top ruins of Corfe Castle which stand sentinel over the Isle of Purbeck, on the Dorset coast, are said to contain a large quantity of hidden wealth, dating from the time of the Civil War. The castle was held by a party of Royalists, under the leadership of Lady Mary Banks, but after a siege lasting two months it fell to Cromwell's troops through the treachery of a Royalist officer. Before surrendering, however, Lady Mary threw all her gold and silver valuables into the castle well, and it is said that the treasure was never recovered.

In Cornwall there is hardly a parish within earshot of the sea that does not boast of its smugglers' or wreckers' hoard ; and in many cases a little investigation will show that these tales are indeed well founded. Take as an example the case of the Gunwalloe treasure, for which many people still dig and search to this day. It dates from the year 1526, when the first of an 'uncanny' series of wrecks occurred on the treacherous stretch of shore between Looe Bar and Halzaphron Cliffs. Of course, wrecks were not unusual on that part of the coast in those days, but what made these rather strange was the fact that all the ships which foundered were carrying large quantities of bullion. In view of this it is not surprising to learn that false lights were blamed for the disasters.

It is significant, perhaps, that when the 1526 wreck occurred 'three Cornish gentlemen', with a large party of retainers, arrived on the scene with suspicious promptness. They saved most of the crew, but—so they later declared—failed to save any of the precious cargo, except a negligible quantity of money which they obtained from the captain. One of the survivors, however, gave testimony later to the effect that most of the bullion had been saved, too, and concealed higher up the beach.

It was also near Gunwalloe Cove that the pirate Captain Emery is said to have buried his hoard. Many local inhabitants, a little more precise than the guide-books, declare that there are actually two hiding-places, one somewhere on the western shores of Looe Pool, and the other near the head of Carminow Creek. Legend also has it that the various treasures hidden around this sparsely populated part of the Lizard Peninsula amount to millions of pounds, when one takes into consideration the present-day value of gold.

Such fabulous wealth, however, is hardly likely to come to the likes of you and me. But small finds occur frequently all over the country, and are almost as exciting as the big ones for those directly concerned. For instance, not very long ago, in my West Dorset village of Chideock, a local farm-hand happened upon a gold archangel, dating from the reign of Henry the Eighth, while ditching in a field at the top of my own cider apple orchard. Needless to say, there ensued quite a local boom in archaeology and excavating!

Indeed, in recent times treasure trove has been discovered on several occasions within a few miles radius of our long-shore village, and there in no reason to suppose that we have been more fortunate in this respect than people on other parts of the coast. A prolonged spell of rain and south-westerly gales sent a cascade of Roman silver coins tumbling down the cliffs between Eype and Bridport Harbour ; whilst in the old Roman county town of Dorchester, shortly before the Second World War, no less than 22,000 silver coins were unearthed by workmen digging foundations for a new store in the High Street. In the old-world village of Burton Bradstock, which lies within earshot of the sea waves clawing at the Chesil Beach, a mystifying treasure was discovered in a disused shaving-stick container which, when opened, was crammed with 100 golden sovereigns. Most of the villagers believed that this hoard must have belonged to an old man of the district, who had died without telling anyone where he had hidden his savings.

In the days of sail the Chesil Beach was a veritable death-trap for shipping, and not for nothing was the vast sweep of coastline between the Bill of Portland and Start Point known as Deadman's Bay. Several treasure ships have been wrecked on this great bank of shingle, including—so it is said—two vessels of the Spanish Armada. This story was to some extent substantiated by the discovery, years ago, of an Armada treasure chest buried in the pebbles of the beach.

At any rate, it is certain that in December, 1641, the *Golden Grape* was stranded here with a rich cargo of wines, silks and bullion. Several days elapsed before the seas finally broke up the stricken vessel, and the local longshore folk made full use of this wonderful opportunity to increase their riches. It is said that to this day there are a number of apparently humble families living in the district who are, in fact, the possessors of considerable wealth—a legacy handed down through the centuries from this and other wrecks.

The richest prize to fall into the hands of the Chesil Beach longshoremen, however, was the *Hope of Amsterdam,* which was driven ashore with £50,000 in jewels and bullion aboard her. The locals helped themselves to much of this before troops appeared on the scene to guard the wreck ; the spoils being secretly buried under cover of darkness to await recovery later when the hue and cry had died down. There were many, however, who were not content with the riches they had already accumulated, and when word got around that the vessel had also been carrying a cargo of spirits the more reckless individuals banded together and carried out raids upon the wreck. For nearly a fortnight pitched battles raged on the beach between troops and gangs of drunken longshoremen, and there were several deaths. Just what happened to the treasure that had been hidden by those men who died we cannot say, because at the time the local inhabitants were naturally very reticent about the whole affair. But tradition says that some of the hoards were never located, and that they still await some lucky finder.

To this day a gold ring or coin from one of these wrecks still sometimes comes the way of the person who wanders

Reverse sides of a Spanish silver piastre, known as 'piece of eight', 1762

along this stretch of coast when tide and shore conditions are right. One old seine-net fisherman found quite a number during his lifetime, and it was a strange experience to finger these centuries-old relics, and wonder at the fate of the men who once owned and coveted them.

So, you see, the unexpected does occasionally happen, and the term 'treasure trove' does sometimes take a rather personal turn. True, the odds of success are long, but scarcely more so, I imagine, than in a large sweepstake. Moreover, for those who turn their week-end excursions into treasure hunts there are bound to be consolation prizes in plenty. Almost invariably the stretches of wild and lovely shore around which legends of hidden treasure have been woven are in themselves beautiful and full of interest.

After all, you know, there are other forms of riches besides gold and silver, diamonds and rubies. Have you never heard of those priceless things called scenic gems? But of course you have! This island of ours is simply studded with them!

Most people nowadays think of smuggling in terms of goods being secretly brought into the country, but it so happens that most of the early instances of smuggling were concerned with an illicit export trade. In the late Middle Ages English wool was in great demand on the Continent, and the English kings of that time were not slow to see in this a likely source of revenue. So a tax was imposed on every bag of wool leaving the country. If they had been modest in their demands all would have been well, but the tax steadily increased, until by the year 1298 the equivalent of about £10 in present-day currency was being levied on every bag of wool bound for foreign ports. This was a crippling burden for the sheep farmers, and it comes as no great surprise when we learn that, about this time, Edward I began to complain bitterly that thousands of bags of wool were being shipped every year from the beaches of Kent and Sussex without payment of duty.

The smugglers who worked at this clandestine export trade were known as 'owlers', presumably because they went about their business during the hours of darkness. For the most part these smuggling gangs consisted of fishermen, who worked in close co-operation with the sheep farmers of the South Downs and Romney Marsh. The farmers, in addition to handling their own wool, would collect consignments from places far inland, and then hand them over to the fishermen for shipment.

During the fourteenth century strenuous efforts were made to open up an English cloth-making industry with the assistance of Flemish weavers, and to aid this scheme the export tax on wool was raised again. At one period, in fact, the export of wool was forbidden altogether. This naturally put the English sheep farmers completely at the mercy of the cloth-makers, who were able to dictate their own terms. As might be expected, the owling trade thrived greatly under these unfair conditions, although the cloth-makers made repeated requests to the authorities to stamp it out. In 1662 offenders were threatened with the gallows if they persisted in 'stealing wool out of the country', but it had little or no effect, and our longshore fishermen cheerfully continued to ferry illicit cargoes of wool across the Channel for anyone who made it worth their while to do so.

The truth of the matter is that the risk of being caught was almost negligible; public sympathy was all on the side of the smugglers, and the Customs officers were hopelessly outnumbered. Indeed, it would be no exaggeration to say that at this period it was the Customs officials, rather than the owlers, who ran the risks. Later on, the Government reinforced their preventive patrols by stationing companies of soldiers at strategic points along the coast, but it is doubtful whether this stratagem gave the owlers much cause for alarm. One of the few results seems to have been a bill for £200, footed by the Treasury, for supplying soldiers with a special issue of shoes and stockings—the normal issue having been 'worn out in the pursuit of smugglers'.

When eventually the owling trade did begin to decline it was not so much due to the activities of the Customs patrols as to a lessening demand for English wool from abroad. Fortunately for the smugglers, however, this more or less coincided with a heavy increase in Customs duties on wines, spirits, tea, tobacco, silks and lace, and in consequence they were able to switch over to the illicit importing of these commodities. Deal and Folkestone—then little more than fishing villages—took a notoriously vigorous part in this 'free-trading', as it was popularly called, and the inhabitants of those places practically lived for smuggling alone.

As a matter of fact my ancestors were Deal fishermen, and I know for certain that our family continued to make nocturnal trips to the French coast until well into the last century. Our house in the old quarter of Deal, which my mother knew as a girl, had access to the beach by a secret underground tunnel; and in case representatives of the law should pay us an unexpected visit there was an emergency escape route, through a cupboard with a false back, into the house next door. Indeed, it would not be incorrect to say that old waterside Deal was designed and built by smugglers for smuggling.

As a security measure the Kentish smugglers never addressed one another by their proper names when engaged on a run, for in the darkness there was always a risk that some eavesdropper might be lurking nearby. Instead, every man was referred to by a nickname, known only to his confederates.

It was the smugglers of Deal who perfected a galley, known as a 'Death', which was rowed with as many as twelve or fourteen oars, and sometimes carried two sails. These boats were so fast that they were able to show a clean pair of heels to any Government blockade vessel that tried to intercept them, and there were many instances of these craft making the double voyage to France and back in a single night. Another advantage of these galleys was their shallow draught, which allowed them to creep up shallow, unguarded waterways to unload their cargoes some distance inland.

So successful was this small-boat smuggling that the Government grew desperate, and began to apply drastic measures. By 1721, so far as sailing craft were concerned, it had been made illegal to use anything but a deep-draught vessel of forty tons burthen or more, even when engaged in properly authorised trading. The many-oared galleys were also declared illegal, and the following notice was posted in all longshore communities around the British coasts:

'Any boat built to row with more than four oars, found upon land or water within the counties of Middlesex, Surrey, Kent or Sussex, or in the River Thames, or within the limits of the ports of London, Sandwich, or Ipswich, or any boat rowing with more than six oars found either upon land or water, in any other port, or within two leagues of the coast of Great Britain, shall be forfeited, and every person using or rowing in such boat shall forfeit £40.'

Other harsh restrictive measures followed in quick succession, and in 1745 anybody found loitering within five miles of the seashore, or a navigable river, was liable to be arrested as a smuggling suspect. No other proof of guilt was necessary, and the punishment meted out might be a severe whipping, followed by a month's hard labour. In the following year an equally grave injustice was inflicted upon those who lived near the coast when county authorities were compelled to foot the bill for losses of revenue due to smuggling within their boundaries. In addition, every instance in which contraband was seized and afterwards recaptured by the free-traders cost the county £200 ; whilst fines of £100 and £40 respectively were imposed whenever a revenue officer was killed or injured in the execution of his duties. The intention behind the imposition of these general fines was obviously to turn public opinion against the smugglers, and encourage informers. However, as practically everyone benefited from the smuggling trade these new laws did not have any very marked effect upon the quantities of contraband brought into the country.

After this the revenue authorities had the bright idea of allowing the crews of certain merchant vessels to arm themselves for the purpose of conducting a private war against the smugglers. These privateers, as they were called, were to receive no regular payment from the Treasury, but whenever they intercepted, seized and handed over a cargo of contraband they were to be rewarded by the Government according to the value of their capture. In theory this was an excellent scheme ; but, as might be expected, quite a number of privateers took advantage of their semi-official position to set up in business as smugglers on their own account. In this way they enjoyed an almost complete immunity from suspicion ; for, even if they were seached by a revenue ship and contraband was found on board, no charge could be upheld against them. To clear themselves they had only to declare that their illicit cargo had been taken from some other vessel in the normal course of their privateering duties. Small wonder, then, that hundreds of incorrigible free-traders suddenly decided to 'reform', and became privateers instead!

In the early days of smuggling the tussles between the revenue men and the free-traders were mostly 'good clean fun', and usually no great harm befell a party of riding officers if they happened to appear on the scene when smuggling operations were in progress. They might receive some rough handling, but as a rule the smugglers would good-naturedly truss them up, make them reasonably comfortable, and then leave them to be found by some passer-by the following morning.

As time went on, however, tempers on both sides grew shorter, and some ugly deeds were perpetrated. History shows that the fishermen who conveyed the goods across the water generally acted with restraint when it came to a fight, and it was not often that they used firearms. Unfortunately, the professional ruffians who were employed to carry smuggled goods from the landing beaches to inland hiding-places rarely had any such scruples, and many of these gangs brought murder to a fine and terrible art.

The most notorious of these smuggling bands was the Hawkhurst gang, which by the seventeen-forties had attained the proportions of a private army. Although named after an inland Sussex village, which they used as a sort of headquarters, the gang operated all along the coast from Kent to East Dorset. The entire countryside went in terror of them, for the leaders of the gang were great believers in the old saying that 'dead men tell no tales', and the inhabitants of village and hamlet took great care not to display any curiosity in their activities. Kipling summed up the situation very aptly when he penned his familiar 'Smugglers' Song':

> If you wake at midnight and hear a horse's feet,
> Don't go drawing back the blind, or looking in the street,
> Them that asks no questions isn't told a lie.
> Watch the wall, my darling, while the Gentlemen go by!
>   Five and twenty ponies,
>   Trotting through the dark—

Brandy for the Parson,
'Baccy for the Clerk ;
Laces for a lady ; letters for a spy,
And watch the wall, my darling, while the Gentlemen go
by!

One daring escapade of the Hawkhurst gang was the historic raid upon the Customs House at Poole, in Dorset, which occurred in October, 1747. A day or two before this exploit was carried out a smuggling cutter belonging to the gang had been captured off Bournemouth. The vessel, which was called the *Three Brothers,* had been carrying a particularly rich cargo of contraband, consisting of nearly two tons of tea and several dozen casks of brandy and rum. The *Three Brothers* was taken into Poole Harbour by the revenue cutter that had made the capture, and the seized goods unloaded from her and placed in the Customs House on the quay.

The Hawkhurst gang were extremely vexed by this loss, and decided to win back their spoils at all costs. So, after a brief parley, sixty of them, mounted on horseback and carrying firearms, made their way to Poole. At close on midnight on October 6th they arrived at their destination, and, while half the party kept a look-out along roads leading into the town, the remaining thirty men battered down the door of the Customs House and recovered the seized contraband. After this they made their way back towards the New Forest, passing through Fordingbridge the following morning.

As they rode through the little town one of the smugglers recognised an erstwhile workmate of his standing amongst a crowd of onlookers, and taking a bag of tea from his saddle he tossed it towards his friend. Daniel Chater was the name of the recipient of this gift, and as he was a poor man he was no doubt delighted with his unexpected windfall. Unfortunately, he was also rather simple-minded, and instead of keeping quiet about the affair he went around telling people that he was hand-in-glove with one of the smugglers. Of course, it was only a matter of time before the authorities got to hear about this, and when they did they promptly took Chater into custody so that they could use him to identify any suspects who might fall into their hands. Eventually, Chater was sent to Chichester, in company with a riding officer called William Galley, to submit his evidence to the local Commissioner of Customs.

What happened next makes gruesome reading, and was the result of a strange twist of fate. For, by some evil chance, during their ride to Chichester the two men took a wrong turning, and while being directed back to their proper route they called at the 'White Hart Inn' at Rowlands Castle. The public-house was kept by a widow whose two sons were both members of the Hawkhurst gang, and becoming suspicious of her customers she sent for some of the smugglers. These men managed to get Daniel Chater by himself for a few minutes, and without much difficulty they persuaded the simple fellow to tell them why he happened to be travelling around in company with a revenue officer.

The smugglers quickly realised that if Chater was allowed to give his evidence they would be in grave danger, and after some discussion they decided to murder him and the revenue officer. But the killing of these two men was no quick, efficient affair. First of all their faces were gouged with spurred boots; after which they were whipped until the floor of the inn kitchen was running with blood. Then the two men, with their legs tied together, were slung over the back of a horse and driven along country lanes to another smugglers' inn, the 'Red Lion', at Rake. This entailed a journey of some twelve miles, and for the entire distance the two helpless men were whipped and belaboured by the smugglers. When eventually they lost consciousness their bodies slid sideways until they hung upside-down beneath the horse's belly, supported by their roped legs. At the end of the journey the revenue officer had been reduced to a mass of shredded and bleeding flesh; whilst the plight of Chater was scarcely better. In due course a hole was dug in a fox-earth on the slopes of nearby Harting Combe, and into this William Galley was bundled and the earth shovelled in on top of him. That he was buried alive was shown by the position of the body when it was discovered some eight months later, the hands being cupped about the nose and mouth as though in a last despairing effort to escape suffocation.

The murderers now returned to the 'Red Lion', and during the next day or two Chater, who was chained by the leg in a nearby shed, received visits from them. One member of the gang, a man called Tapner, subjected the prisoner to fiendish tortures, forcing him to kneel and recite the Lord's Prayer while he had his face slashed with a knife. After that Chater's eyes were put out, and he was taken to Ladyholt Park, near South Harting. There, with a noose about his neck, he was suspended over a disused well and slowly strangled. Before he was quite dead, however, they let go of the rope and allowed him to fall to the bottom of the shaft, believing that this would kill him. A spark of life still flickered in his mangled body, however, and as Chater's tormentors were about to leave they heard an agonised groan issue from the depths of the well. They dared not leave their victim alive, in case he was discovered and lingered long enough to give evidence against them. So they dropped large stones and heavy fencing posts on to him until he had been silenced for good.

It is a relief to learn that seven of the murderers were brought to trial and condemned to death at Chichester the following year. The body of the sadistic Tapner was hanged in chains on Rook's Hill, near Chichester; whilst others were displayed in similar fashion near the scene of the murders, and on the coast, near Selsey Bill.

The punishment meted out to these men did not deter the other smugglers, however, and all along the coast shiploads of contraband continued to be run whenever conditions were favourable. The large gangs of inlanders still resorted to murder whenever it suited their purpose, but the smaller longshore confederacies relied mainly upon their native wit to keep them clear of the law. Perhaps this was because the sailors had not quite so much at stake. Their seamanship was of great value to the country, and when convicted of a smuggling offence they were usually condemned to a compulsory period of service in the Royal Navy—from which they frequently succeeded in escaping within a few months. The 'useless' inland smugglers, on the other hand, often finished up by being hanged at Execution Dock, near Deptford, and in consequence they would go to desperate lengths to avoid capture.

Captain Brenton, writing about the qualities of the English sea-smuggler in his *History of the Royal Navy,* tells us that these men were 'as remarkable for their skill in seamanship as for their audacity in the hour of danger'. He also adds, 'They are hardy, sober, and faithful to each other, beyond the generality of seamen; and, when shipwreck occurs, have been known to perform deeds not exceeded in any country in the world; probably unequalled in the annals of other maritime powers.' Elsewhere it is recorded that members of the smuggling fraternity, when sent to serve in the Navy, were often promoted over the heads of the less seamanlike pressed men and volunteers—to the discontent of the latter.

The ruses employed by smugglers to avoid detection were many. If the Customs officers were unduly active on a night when a run of contraband was due, the smugglers' vessel would be 'flashed off' with a dark lantern. The tubs of spirits would then be sunk some distance offshore and their position buoyed. Next day, when 'the coast was clear', the tubs would be retrieved by the local fishermen, and brought ashore hidden amongst their nets. When the revenue men learnt of this, and began searching for the buoys themselves, the smugglers began to disguise their buoys to look like pieces of drifting flotsam. On one occasion, however, a particularly astute revenue man, while standing on the shore, noticed a gull's feather floating on the water. In spite of the fact that a fair breeze was blowing at the time, the feather lay motionless, and this aroused the man's suspicions. Swimming out to investigate, he found that the feather was attached by a length of fishing line to a sunken raft of kegs—and so the smugglers had to think up another fresh idea.

All along the south coast, from Kent to Cornwall, church towers and churchyard tombs served the free-traders as hiding-places for their smuggled goods. The peculiar, pagoda-shaped bell tower of Brookland Church, on Romney Marsh, was used for this purpose, and it is even said that a certain parson of Brookland appointed himself as custodian of the illicit cellar!

To deter the curiosity of those who might think it strange

The peculiar, pagoda-shaped bell tower of Brookland Church, on Romney Marsh

that lights should be flickering back and forth among the tombstones in the middle of the night, the smugglers often put about tales that these will-o'-the-wisp illuminations were due to supernatural causes. Some smuggling gangs even 'laid on' their own ghost, rubbing one of their company with phosphorus and encouraging him to wander around the

176

precincts of the church, uttering strange and unearthly noises. Derelict buildings were also used by the smugglers as hiding-places for their goods, and numbered among these was Hurstmonceux Castle, in Sussex, which during the eighteenth and nineteenth centuries was a deserted ruin. This is supposed to have been the origin of the phantom drummer of Hurstmonceux Castle, who paraded up and down the ramparts whenever a run of contraband was being made in the district.

The unusual detached church tower at Talland, in Cornwall, was another smugglers' cellar. So it is probably no mere coincidence that in the eighteenth century the place was haunted o' nights by a veritable army of demons. Parson Dodge, who lived in the adjoining rectory, is said to have spent much of his time chasing these evil spirits around his churchyard. It is more likely, though, that the spirits Parson Dodge pursued so energetically were of an alcoholic nature —and that he was afraid the 'demons' would try to cheat him out of his allotted tithe of kegs!

One of the best-known stories of a smuggling ruse comes to us from a certain village in Wiltshire. Although this county has no seaboard, the coastline around Christchurch and Bournemouth is not far distant, and in the heyday of smuggling, illicit goods were conveyed into Wiltshire in considerable quantities. Consequently, the county received a fair amount of attention from the revenue authorities, and one night, when the moon was full, a party of riding officers surprised a number of rustics dabbling with hayrakes in the waters of a village pond.

'What are you doing there?' demanded the senior officer, suspiciously.

A deceptively simple-looking old man, who had been on the point of raking a keg of brandy from its hiding-place under the muddy water, slowly straightened his back and treated the horseman to a foolish grin. Then, jerking his thumb to indicate the reflection of the full moon shimmering on the surface of the pond, he declared. 'Why, zur, us were jest a-tryin' to rake thick yer girt cheese out o' the water.'

The revenue men, roaring with laughter at this display of rustic simple-mindedness, rode on their way—leaving the equally delighted smugglers to recover their kegs of brandy undisturbed. And to this day the people of those parts, not without a touch of pride, still refer to themselves as 'Wiltshire Moonrakers'.

A number of extremely colourful smuggling personalities held sway along the south coast during the late eighteenth and early nineteenth centuries. Such a character was Isaac Gulliver, who lived at Kinson, near Poole, in Dorset. 'Old Gulliver' as he was affectionately known to his men, had a remarkable flair for organisation, and was probably the most successful smuggler of all time. He owned several fast luggers; ran a small private army of bodyguards, and amassed a very considerable fortune, of which over £80,000 still remained when he died at a ripe old age. He was a model employer, and dressed his men, both ashore and afloat, in a sort of livery. He also issued them with hair powder, so that they could wear their hair long and white, in the fashionable 'gentleman's gentleman' style of those days. This earned them the title of 'White Wigs' among the other smugglers.

Gulliver's boats made regular contraband runs to the shores around Lyme Regis, Weymouth, Poole and Christchurch, but his favourite landing-places were the sandy hollows, known as 'chines', which are a feature of the coast near Bournemouth. In those days, of course, Bournemouth was little more than a lonely longshore fishing settlement.

For his success as a free-trader Old Gulliver relied almost entirely upon organisation and strategy, and his men had strict instructions to act with restraint should they ever come to blows with the revenue men. For this reason bloodshed was rare, and murder unheard of, in the lengthy history of the White Wigs. It was a policy which the authorities apparently appreciated, for on the few occasions when any of Gulliver's men were captured they were treated more leniently than the general run of free-traders.

Another outstanding smuggling personality was Thomas Johnson, who was born in 1772. Quite early in life he fell foul of the revenue men and was thrown into gaol, but he contrived to escape shortly afterwards, and a reward of £500 was offered for his recapture. To put himself on better terms with the authorities, therefore, Johnson volunteered to act as pilot to a British expedition that was shortly to be sent against the French in Holland. General Sir Ralph Abercromby, who was organising the venture, gladly agreed to make use of his services, and, in return, recommended that the smuggler should be pardoned for his previous crimes.

The pardon was duly granted, but it did not do Johnson much good. By 1802 he had fallen heavily into debt, and rather ignominiously he was sent to cool his heels in the Fleet debtors' prison. However, on a dark November night he decided to make a bid for freedom. As a sailor he was naturally an agile climber, and by making use of a few finger and toe holds in the masonry of the tall prison wall he managed to scale it. There was a tremendous drop on the other side into the public street, though, and Johnson realised that he would have to break his fall in some way if he were to avoid injury. So he crawled along the top of the wall until he was directly above an iron lamp-bracket, which overhung the footwalk. By his finger-tips he lowered himself slowly, and then allowed himself to drop on to the bracket. By a mischance he failed to notice a jagged piece of metal which protruded from the stanchion, and this caught in his leg, ripping the flesh wide open. He cursed his luck; then caught his breath suddenly as a watchman, carrying a lantern, came walking slowly down the street. Johnson, with the blood from his wound dripping on to the pavement below, froze along the crossbar of the lamp-bracket, expecting every second to hear the watchman's challenge ring out upon the silent night. But the man trudged by with downcast gaze, and as soon as he had passed out of sight the smuggler dropped into the street and hastened away to contact some of his friends. With their help he escaped to the Continent—where he was promptly arrested and flung into gaol by some of Napoleon's henchmen.

Johnson was sorely puzzled by this unkind reception; for as a rule English smugglers, as enemies of the British

Government, enjoyed the hospitality of the French Republic, even when the two countries were at war. Before long, though, Johnson was told the reason for his arrest. Napoleon, it appeared, was planning an attack upon the shores of England, and he was willing to allow Johnson to earn his freedom by piloting the French invasion fleet through the intricacies of the English coastal waters. Johnson refused to have any truck with the scheme, and his angry captors put him to rot in a dark and filthy dungeon. This might well have been his fate, too ; but after nine months he managed to escape, and took ship for America, unaware that meanwhile the British Government had pardoned his past transgressions.

Perhaps this unusual forgiveness on the part of the authorities was due to the fact that they were again eager to use his skill as a pilot. At any rate, three years later he was acting in that capacity with the Royal Navy off the west coast of France. Moreover, his services were sufficiently noteworthy to warrant his being mentioned in despatches.

When the fleet returned to port he went back to smuggling for another two or three years. Then, apparently considering it about time that he earned himself another pardon, he volunteered to act as pilot to the ill-starred Walcheren Expedition. On this disastrous enterprise he conducted himself so well that, in addition to the free pardon that had been promised to him, he was presented with an annual pension of £100.

Thomas Johnson's life took several unusual turns during its remaining thirty years. But perhaps the most remarkable episode was when this smuggler-cum-pilot got bitten by the inventing bug, and accepted a commission from the Spanish Government to construct a submarine. He duly built the primitive craft ; testing it on the Thames amongst the shipping anchored between Wapping and Blackwall Reach. On one occasion, while the submarine was cruising along beneath the surface of the river, it became ensnared in a ship's anchor chains, and Johnson and his crew nearly lost their lives.

The most exciting smuggling career of all, however, must

surely have been that of Jack Rattenbury, who was a native of the little Devonshire fishing village of Beer. Unlike the other free-traders, he kept written records of all his exploits, and from these we are able to gain an exciting glimpse into the hard and adventurous lives of the West Country smuggling fraternity.

Writing about his family background, Rattenbury tells us that he was born in 1778, and adds that shortly before this happy event took place his father, a shoemaker by trade, went aboard a British man-o'-war and was never heard of again. At the age of nine, young Jack joined the crew of his uncle's fishing boat. One day, when left in sole charge of the boat, he was unlucky enough to lose the rudder, and for this unseamanlike behaviour his uncle treated him to such a lavish taste of a rope's-end that he ran away to become apprentice to a Brixham fisherman. However, he very soon found that he received even harsher treatment from the other apprentices, all of whom were older than himself, and after enduring his unhappy lot for a year he returned to Beer.

Fishing being none too profitable, and war having broken out between England and France, his uncle had by that time decided to throw in his lot with a crew of privateers, and he took the lad with him. For several months they quartered the seas, searching in vain for a suitable enemy vessel to plunder. Eventually they came up with a ship flying the British flag, and in an extravagant display of patriotism the privateer captain ordered all hands aloft to give the other crew three cheers. Unfortunately for the men of Beer, however, the 'English' ship turned out to be a Frenchman sailing under false colours, and armed with no less than twenty-six concealed guns. The result was that, instead of falling victim to the privateers, she finished up by capturing them.

The Englishmen were clapped in irons and landed at Bordeaux, where they were thrown into gaol. Young Jack Rattenbury, however, contrived to escape by a cunning ruse, and hid himself aboard an American ship that was destined to lay a year in the harbour before being permitted to sail. Eventually the vessel put to sea, and forty-five days later the boy arrived in New York. From there he took ship for Havre de Grace, and then at that port signed on with another vessel bound, as he thought, for London; but, instead, he found himself in Copenhagen. At last, after being stormbound for three months in a Norwegian fjord, he arrived at Guernsey, and from there returned to his native Beer.

For a while he earned a meagre living by longshore fishing, but his boyhood adventures had given him a taste for excitement, and not long after his sixteenth birthday he joined the crew of a smuggling vessel which made regular runs between Alderney and Lyme Regis. Next, at Bridport, he joined an honest coasting vessel called *The Friends,* bound for Tenby, but during the course of the voyage they were captured by a French privateer.

Things looked black, but young Jack was equal to the situation and, when entrusted by a drunken French officer with the helm of the captured ship, ignored his orders and steered close in to the Dorset coast. Off Swanage he leapt overboard and swam for the shore, afterwards raising an alarm that enabled a revenue cutter to intercept *The Friends* and bring her safely back to port.

If this praiseworthy act on the part of Jack Rattenbury earned the gratitude of the authorities they did not show it; instead, they press-ganged him into the Royal Navy. However, this was a small matter for the youth and, after giving the Navy a fortnight's trial, he made himself scarce and went cod-fishing off Newfoundland. Returning home from this voyage he was again captured by privateers—they were Spaniards this time—and his voyage ended at Vigo.

By making full use of his native wit, Rattenbury regained his liberty and returned to Beer. By this time he was about twenty-three years of age, and still an eligible bachelor. But this state of affairs did not last long, for on a spring day in 1801 he married a local girl. She was a devil-may-care lass, always ready to assist her husband in his numerous escapades. Once, at Bridport, she tackled single-handed a naval lieutenant and his press-gang of nine men as they pursued

Rattenbury along the waterfront. The lieutenant threw the girl to the ground, whereupon the local townspeople, their sense of chivalry outraged, joined battle with the hated press-gang while Rattenbury quietly made good his escape.

Family responsibilities proved to be a drain on his financial resources, so privateering and smuggling began to attract him once more. Rattenbury never had any success as a privateer, but smuggling proved quite profitable, and he landed many cargoes of wines and spirits on Beer beach, concealing them beneath his fishing nets. On one of these trips he was captured by a revenue cutter, but escaped by hiding himself in the bilge of the Government boat and making a remarkable dash to freedom the instant they reached land. Until nightfall he lay in hiding; then, under cover of darkness, he returned to the cutter and rescued, not only his imprisoned friends, but also some of their captured cargo. Such was the mettle of Jack Rattenbury, ace smuggler and will-o'-the-wisp.

The following year he again fell foul of the revenue authorities, and was drafted into the Navy as punishment. He escaped by leaping overboard from the ship to which he had been posted; afterwards returning to his old occupation of smuggling. He and some of his friends bought a fast galley and carried out several profitable cognac runs from the Channel Islands to Beer—a distance of nearly one hundred miles each way. They were risky voyages to make in such a light craft, and eventually the galley was wrecked during a gale. Nothing daunted, Rattenbury and a companion decided to make another contraband trip in a small rowing boat, but on the return voyage they were picked up by a Government vessel and landed at Falmouth to stand trial for smuggling. Sent by chaise from Falmouth to Bodmin Gaol, the two prisoners got their guards drunk and made good their escape. Later, back home in Beer, Rattenbury was cornered in a cellar by a sergeant and ten privates, all armed with swords and muskets. The redoubtable smuggler, however, picked up a reaping hook and held this small army at bay for four hours. Indeed, he might have remained there longer had not some of the local fisher-girls learned of his

183

predicament. They burst in upon the soldiers with a fictitious story about a shipwreck, so that for a second everyone's attention was diverted from the hunted man. That second was all Rattenbury needed. He leapt out of the cellar, raced down to the shore, and was off to sea in his boat before the soldiers had finally disengaged themselves from the clutches of the women.

Puck-faced and merry, Jack Rattenbury certainly had a way with the ladies; possibly because he rarely forgot to include a consignment of lace and silks among his cargoes of contraband. On one occasion, during a run from Cherbourg, a batch of lace was hidden inside the carcase of a goose.

One of Jack's feminine admirers was Lady Rolle, who more than once prevailed upon her husband to use his influence on Rattenbury's behalf when the smuggler was being threatened by the law. He certainly needed her patronage, for he was not a lucky smuggler, and his schemes were forever going awry. Yet he had an almost miraculous gift for wriggling out of his difficulties, and although arrested times without number he continued to indulge in his free-trading activities until nearly sixty years of age. Finally, he retired on a small pension granted by Lord and Lady Rolle, and left his smuggler son to carry on the 'family business'.

Nowadays much of the old romance and vigour has gone out of smuggling, although the business of 'free-trading' is still carried on. Occasionally, however, a modern smuggling gang recaptures something of the reckless spirit of the past, as did the crew of a motor cruiser shortly after the Second World War. Encouraged by inflated prices for wines and spirits, due to shortages in Britain, a Canadian ex-Naval officer organised a series of audacious runs to various parts of the English coast. Much ingenuity was needed to buy the large quantities of liquor on the Continent without arousing suspicion, and on one occasion two of the smugglers, when visiting a French wine merchant, posed as officers from the battleship, H.M.S. *Vanguard*. They told the merchant that they were purchasing large stocks of liqueurs for a forthcoming Royal visit to South Africa, and persuaded the excited Frenchman to keep quiet about the transaction in order to avoid arousing the jealousy of his business rivals.

Towards the end of his career, in 1947, the leader of the smugglers devised a scheme in which his motor cruiser was intercepted at night by another section of his gang in an ex-Government invasion barge. The contraband was then transferred from the cruiser to the shallow-draught barge, and landed on the shores of a deserted creek near Poole. Only a careless slip on the part of a woman associate of the gang gave the clue for which the Customs had been waiting, and shortly afterwards, with the assistance of the Dorset police, a number of the gang were caught red-handed with a huge consignment of liquor on the shores of Poole Harbour. The remainder of the gang were rounded up shortly afterwards, and all were tried at Wareham, in Dorset. Apart from a number of prison sentences, and the confiscation of their boat, fines were imposed on the smugglers which amounted to more than £18,000.

'Oh, it's all right for some people, I daresay, but give me a nice soft bed to sleep in,' is the sort of exasperating reply I often receive when I begin to eulogise the pleasures of holi-daying with a tent.

Fortunately, for every unenlightened diehard who (quite erroneously) insists upon regarding camping as a form of 'roughing it', there are usually several people who are eager to give the pastime a fair trial. Provided they go about things in the right way, these newcomers to camping soon dis-cover that living under canvas is the ideal method of spend-ing a seaside holiday. It is as cheap as living at home; it is healthy; and, above all, it means freedom from all those petty restrictions normally associated with a seaside boarding house.

For instance, when camping it is possible to adjust meal-times to suit one's own convenience. If you and your family happen to be ardent rock-pool enthusiasts there will be no need for you to trudge back at midday to a landlady's boiled beef and carrots, just when the tide is exactly right for prawning and the lobsters are nibbling at your bait. Instead, when the tide has turned, you can light a driftwood fire on the beach, put on a cooking-pot filled with sea water, and before long everyone will be sitting down to a veritable banquet of boiled lobsters, crabs and prawns.

Having whetted your appetite for seaside camping, let us now consider some of those problems which face the newcomer to the pastime. The type of tent and equipment you will require depends largely upon your mode of travel when on holiday. Walkers and cyclists should choose a small tent made of proofed Egyptian cotton, and the groundsheet, made to fit the tent, should be as light and compact as pos-sible. Cooking utensils may take the form of a composite canteen, incorporating frying-pan, boiling-pot, and plate.

Other requirements are quite modest: a kapok- or eider-down-filled sleeping-bag (blankets are a very second best, and far more bulky and heavy); a canvas water bucket; a jack-knife, incorporating a tin opener; a small paraffin pressure stove and a few lightweight food containers.

Both walkers and cyclists will find that it pays to give some earnest thought to the question of carrying their kit. Although presenting no real problem, it is nevertheless surprising how many people go wrong on this point. A metal-framed rucksack may be ideal for the person who travels on foot, but for the cyclist it is an instrument of torture. The latter fraternity should make their machines carry the load in a pair of pannier bags strapped to the carrier, and in a large touring bag attached to the saddle. This arrangement keeps the centre of gravity as low as possible, and reduces the additional strain on both cycle and rider to a minimum.

The motorist, of course, can allow himself a lot more scope as regards the weight of his equipment, and will usually include such luxuries as a pressure cooker, folding chairs and table, and camp beds. Even so, the lightweight principle should not be lost sight of entirely; otherwise the car will tend to look—and sound—like a travelling hardware stores.

Good quality camping equipment is not cheap but it pays to buy the best. Although the original outlay may seem rather a lot, it should be remembered that in buying a tent you are buying a lifetime of inexpensive holidays. Old hands at camping shun the large commercialised sites, preferring to pitch down at some quiet, little-known spot on the coast.

Many people on their first camping tour are apt to be a little diffident about asking for permission to pitch their tent for the night. There are, of course, plenty of tracts of open moorland in the country where one may reasonably camp for a single night without seeking permission, but in all other cases you should pay a courtesy call on the landowner before pitching your tent. Rarely indeed will a farmer refuse to let you camp in the place you have in mind, and if he does it will almost certainly be for some good reason, and he will quickly suggest an alternative site.

When choosing a place to pitch your tent the following points—given in the order in which they should be attended to—are the main ones to take into consideration:

(1) Is there a source of safe water at hand for cooking and drinking purposes?

(2) If cooking by fire, is there an adequate supply of dead wood?

(3) If weather conditions are unsettled, is there sufficient shelter from the wind?

(4) Is the surface of the ground suitable—i.e. is it reasonably smooth and level?

(5) Is the nature of the ground below the surface suitable —i.e. is it firm enough to offer a good hold for your tent-pegs in the event of a storm? Is there danger of it becoming waterlogged after prolonged rain?

Having satisfied yourself on these points, pitch your tent with its back to the wind, either on a patch of level, slightly raised ground; or in such a way that your head will be a little higher than your feet. Never, on any account, pitch your tent broadside on to the wind or the slope of a hillside. Apart from these considerations you should also arrange your tent so that it derives as much benefit as possible from any shelter that is going—either from a hedge, wall, hillside or group of trees. Never, however, pitch your tent directly underneath trees in the mistaken impression that in this way they will give you more protection from the elements. Instead, you will be treated to a shower-bath long after a storm of rain has passed away.

Your paraffin pressure stove will prove to be a particularly welcome item of equipment in wet weather. A camp-fire is a perfectly satisfactory method of cooking in fine weather, but the person who puts all his faith in it will soon be reduced to eating cold food if conditions become less kind. Bear in mind, too, that it is not sufficient to have a pressure stove; one must also have the means of lighting it, and boxes of matches are apt to become useless through damp. Consequently, it is a wise plan to carry an emergency supply of red-topped matches, safe from any damp in a tightly corked bottle, with each match head thinly coated with candle-grease so that it may be struck in the open—even in a down-pour of rain.

People who have never done any camping are apt to think that cooking one's own food must be rather a bore. As a matter of fact it can be quite good fun, especially when camping by the sea, where there are excellent opportunities for catching at least some of your own food. We have already seen how the tidal rock pools on many parts of the coast are capable of providing lobsters, crabs, prawns and shellfish. All these need to be cooked in salty water, and it is a point worth noting by longshore campers that there is nothing better for this purpose than the sea water provided by Nature.

Fish make an excellent stand-by, and when caught fresh from the sea bear no resemblance at all to the dull-eyed things to be seen reposing on the inland fishmonger's slab. When camping by the sea, therefore, include some fishing tackle amongst your equipment. If you follow the instructions contained in another chapter of this book you will soon catch your supper. For camp-fire cooking, oily fish, such as mackerel, are most suitable, as these can be grilled over a bed of glowing embers without using any fat. The best method is to spit the fish lengthways on a sliver of green wood, resting the ends of the spit on two Y-shaped pieces of wood stuck into the ground on either side of the fire. The fish should, of course, be turned occasionally during the cooking process. Small non-oily fish, such as pouting, may also be grilled, but they should be lightly greased.

Mention of food calls to mind several wrinkles on open-air cookery which may prove useful to those beginning camping. If using a fire, avoid lighting it too close to the front of your tent. Even when the wind is blowing steadily from behind you, and the risk of a flying spark burning a hole in your tent can be discounted, you will find that eddies of air, set up by the open end of your tent, will carry the smoke back to where you are sitting. Likewise, when actually engaged in cooking at the fire, never crouch with your back to the wind. Instead, position yourself sideways to the wind so that it has free access to the fire, and is thus able to blow away the smoke. It is worth remembering also that the experienced camper boils the water for his tea or coffee while the fire is blazing, and then, when a bed of glowing charcoals has been formed, begins the business of frying or grilling.

All this may sound rather complicated and wearisome to the person toying with the idea of taking a holiday under canvas for the first time. Actually it isn't, and no prospective camper should allow himself to be deterred from giving the pastime a trial simply because good camping amounts to something more than setting up a tent somewhere, crawling into it, and going to sleep. Once a person has mastered the art of camping he will begin to take a pride in his skill at the game, and will even enjoy an occasional storm to prove that skill in a tussle with the elements.

Of course, like everyone else, the experienced camper likes his holidays to be fine and sunny. Nevertheless, he knows that even wild weather has its compensations, especially for those who venture into the lonely places. For it is on some wild and deserted stretch of shore that one gets to know the deep satisfaction of falling asleep to the roar of the surf, the thunder of the under-tow, and the moaning of the night wind among the boulders. There is, too, the thrill of hearing the spine-chilling cry of a baby seal, or the plaintive fluting of curlews flying over the estuary tide-flats. One learns, also, that it is in the lonely places that the green-blue flames of a driftwood fire seem to burn at their brightest; that it is here the voice of a good companion sounds most pleasant, and the inside of a down sleeping-bag feels most snug.

A day of high-spirited fun beside the sea can very quickly change into one of stark tragedy, and during the summer months the beaches, rock pools, cliffs and river estuaries of Britain are the scenes of countless accidents. In nearly every case these accidents need never have happened, being the result of thoughtlessness, recklessness, or ignorance—and not infrequently a combination of all three.

Everybody, for instance, must be aware of the danger of allowing oneself to become cut off by a rising tide ; yet quite intelligent people have been known to fall victim to the sea in this way. The fascinating contents of a rock pool can easily beguile the budding longshore naturalist into forgetting for a while the ever-lurking menace of the rising waters. And the sea, glassy smooth and silent, does nothing to remind him. With small, stealthy surges it encircles the weed-stranded boulders, and fills the deep treacherous gullies between the sand-pits. Every year hundreds of holiday-makers find themselves marooned in this way, and have to be rescued by fishermen or the local lifeboat. Sometimes, on lonely stretches of coast, their predicament goes unnoticed ; and then yet another drowning tragedy finds an inch or so of space in the daily papers.

Everyone, of course, should do their utmost to learn to swim ; although it cannot be stressed too strongly that this accomplishment does not absolve the seaside holidaymaker from taking precautions. It is a sobering fact that more swimmers are drowned around our coasts every year than non-swimmers. Of these ill-fated swimmers, a very large proportion are over-venturesome novices who allow themselves to be caught in a tidal current and swept out to sea. Should you be unlucky enough to find yourself in this predicament you should avoid tiring yourself unnecessarily by fighting against the current. Swim for the shore, of course, but do not worry unduly if, at the same time, you find yourself drifting along the coast. Panic is the thing to guard against ; it has drowned far more people than physical exhaustion.

Needless to say, the more sensible plan is to avoid getting into difficulties. If you are a non-swimmer, find out before venturing into the sea whether the beach shelves gently or steeply. You can do this quite easily by watching people already in the water. Pebble beaches often shelve comparatively gently for some distance, and then plunge abruptly into much deeper water. They can be very dangerous for children and non-swimmers, but are usually quite safe for the swimmer. A surf-swept strand, on the other hand, although shelving gently and uniformly, is often made dangerous for even powerful swimmers by tidal currents and an undertow. In any case, it is always a wise plan to seek local advice before swimming off a strange and little-frequented stretch of coast.

There are many powerful swimmers who like to display their prowess by swimming far out to sea. Unfortunately, even powerful swimmers are not immune to cramp, and quite a number disappear from sight every year with a valedictory gurgle. There is a lot to be said for practising long-distance swimming, but it is best carried out close to the shore.

'Messing about in boats' can be excellent fun, but non-swimmers would be well-advised to refrain from indulging in too much 'messing about' while their boat is at sea. Even swimmers should act with reasonable discretion, especially when in a sailing craft. The boom of even a small sailing dinghy is quite capable of knocking a careless helmsman unconscious before sending him spinning into the sea. Similarly, in the case of a capsized boat, a thole pin can suddenly become a lethal weapon if it happens to come into contact with a person's head.

Another item of a boat's equipment which can be dangerous in unskilled hands is the starting cord of an outboard motor. Its knotted end, suddenly whipping free from the flywheel, is quite capable of putting out the eye of anybody sitting nearby. An arm raised to shield the face is the only precaution necessary.

Such things as rubber dinghies, floats and small canoes have proved the undoing of many an amateur mariner. These flimsy craft are used as a rule when the sea is calm; and the very fact that the sea is calm usually means that the wind is blowing offshore. The voyage out to sea will therefore be all too easy. It is when the time comes to put about and make for the shore again that the trouble will start!

All reasonably strong swimmers should endeavour to make themselves proficient in the various methods of life-saving. Most of these entail use of the 'back-kick', by means of which the rescuer swims on his back, using only his legs to propel himself and the person he is rescuing through the water. The hands, of course, are needed to hold the drowning person's head above water, and in the case of a subject who is panic-stricken and violent this is no easy matter. One of the most effective ways of overcoming this difficulty is for the rescuer to approach the drowning person from behind, thrust his arms under the other's armpits, and then fold his hands across the other's chest. In this way the drowning person is held powerless, whilst at the same time being supported by the body of the rescuer.

Of course, not everyone who is called upon to save a drowning person is an expert at life-saving, and quite often a would-be rescuer finds himself being dragged under by the frantic clutches of the one he is trying to help. A drowning person, however, will loosen his hold if the rescuer climbs on top of him and thrusts him under the water. In carrying out this manœuvre, the rescuer should place his left hand upon the subject's right shoulder; the palm of his right hand against the other's chin, and at the same time bring his right knee up against the lower part of the other's chest (*see* illustration). Then, with a strong and sudden movement, he should stretch his right arm straight out while pulling firmly *downwards* with the left arm. The pull of the left hand should bring the subject under the rescuer so that the pushing action of his right hand and knee is downwards. This

The above illustration shows the rescuer climbing on top of the drowning man, thrusting him under the water, thus forcing him to release his grip

This method of release is to be used when the rescuer is clutched round the arms and body by the drowning person

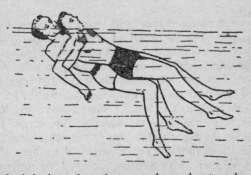

Method for bringing a drowning man ashore who struggles violently

In the case of struggling violently or if the arms be difficult to grasp, slip your hands under the armpits of the drowning person and place them on his chest and with your own arms raise his arms at right angles to his body; then lie on your back and swim with the back stroke

194

sudden motion will break the drowning person's clutch and leave the rescuer unhampered and in control.

Before leaving the subject of life-saving, mention should be made of artificial respiration, which in dictionary terminology is 'the mechanical restoration of the act of breathing when it has been suspended by drowning, suffocation, etc.'. There are several methods of artificial respiration in common use, but the most efficient is almost certainly the very straightforward Holger Nielsen method, recommended by the Royal Life Saving Society. In the Society's Handbook (22nd edition) very lucid instructions are given for restoring life by this means, and this information, very kindly put at my disposal, is given in the following paragraphs, while the diagrams of the Holger Nielsen method are shown on page 197.

HOW TO APPLY THE 'HOLGER NIELSEN' METHOD OF RESUSCITATION WHEN BREATHING HAS APPARENTLY CEASED

To Promote Artificial Breathing, Observe the Following Instructions

PATIENT

Immediately the body of the apparently drowned person is removed from the water, place it in the prone position on the nearest flat surface, if possible with the head slightly lower than the feet. Bend the patient's arms and place his hands one over the other under his forehead. Not an instant is to be lost; quickly loosen any tight neck-band and clear the mouth if necessary; give 2 or 3 smart slaps with the flat hand, between the patient's shoulders, to ensure that his tongue falls forward and to remove any obstruction.

Artificial respiration must begin without a moment's delay and should be kept up as long as any hope exists. In some cases life has been restored after hours of unceasing work.

Operator

Kneel on one knee a little in front of and to the side of the patient's head. Place the other foot with the heel at the side of the patient's elbow. Rest the hands on the patient's shoulder-blades, thumbs on spine and fingers pointing to feet, arms sloping obliquely forward. (Fig. 1.)

Expiration

Rock gently forward on straight arms till nearly vertical: exert no pressure. Count one, two, three in 2 seconds. (Fig. 2.)

Change (*a*)

Rock back, sliding hands over the patient's shoulders until they reach the elbows, counting four.

Inspiration

Raise the patient's arms slightly and pull gently on the backward rock. Counting—five, six, seven in 2 seconds. (Fig. 3.)

Change (*b*)

Lower the patient's arms to the ground and move hands back to the starting position, counting eight. (Fig. 4.)

Continuation

Repeat the cycle 'one' to 'eight', gently and rhythmically till breathing recommences.

After Natural Breathing has been Established Observe the Following Instructions

To promote circulation, rub the inside of the limbs towards the heart with a firm pressure of the hands. Dry the hands and feet, and as soon as dry clothing can be procured, strip the patient and reclothe or cover with blankets. Continue friction over the dry clothing or under the blankets.

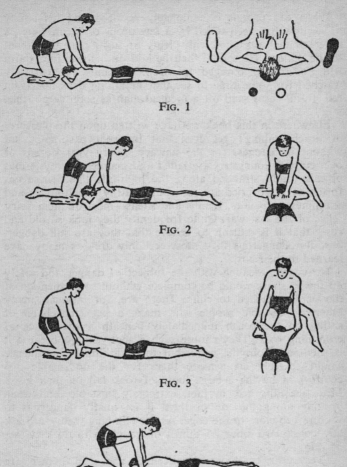

Fig. 1

Fig. 2

Fig. 3

Fig. 4

The Holger Nielsen method of artificial respiration as recommended by The Royal Life Saving Society (see text for procedure)

197

When the patient is completely restored and his ability to swallow has been tested by a few drops of warm water, a little hot tea sweetened with plenty of sugar may be offered to the patient. He should then be laid on his side in a warm bed and be encouraged to sleep. He must be carefully watched for some time to see that breathing does not again fail. In all cases send for a medical man as soon as possible.

Elsewhere in this book we have written upon the pleasures of beachcombing; yet even that innocent pastime is not without its dangers for the unwary. Every year dozens of over-curious youngsters are killed and maimed by mysterious objects found stranded along the high-tide line. These unfortunate discoveries are, of course, stray beach-mines and sea-mines, torpedoes, bombs and shells—most of them being relics of the last war. Quite frequently they look so old and rusty that it is difficult to believe that they are still dangerous. But dangerous they most certainly are—as many have learned to their cost.

No chapter dealing with the subject of danger and safety on the seashore would be complete without some mention of the perils attached to cliffs. There are, for instance, many otherwise sensible people who make a persistent habit of sitting on the beach immediately beneath a sheer face of crumbling rock. They choose such a spot perhaps because it is sheltered from the wind, but this additional convenience would scarcely compensate them for the undeniable discomfort of having a large lump of rock fall on their head. Most sea-cliffs are, in fact, extremely unstable, and when walking along the top of them it is equally dangerous to venture too close to the edge. As for climbing them—just ask any coastguard what he thinks of people who do that sort of thing!

Every year, coastguards, policemen, and even firemen, are called upon to risk their own lives in order to rescue holiday-makers with more energy than sense—people who regard a steep and slippery cliff-face as a heaven-sent medium for making themselves conspicuous. Admittedly, there are a few reasonably experienced mountain climbers who go 'cliffing' for a change when holidaying by the sea, but their numbers are few, and their activities very localised. The fact is that most sea-cliffs possess little attraction for the serious climber. Unlike mountains, which are normally composed of hard rock affording reasonably secure handholds and footholds, the majority of sea-cliffs are composed of such unstable substances as crumbling chalk and sandstone, or slippery clay. Even solid granite, when constantly wetted by salt spray, becomes treacherous for the person wearing rubber soles; whilst unexpected patches of damp and greasy herbage can send an unwary climber plummeting headlong to his doom.

Should you chance to see any people in difficulties on a cliff-face, do not embark rashly on a rescue attempt there and then. Without proper ropes and skilled assistance your gallant gesture could all too easily end in disaster. Instead, shout out to those concerned that help is on the way, and tell them to remain where they are and not to panic. Then hasten away to inform the local coastguards or police, who will almost certainly be better qualified and equipped to deal with such an emergency. If, before the arrival of official help, someone appears on the scene with a rope, this can be lowered to the people in difficulties to help steady them if their position is precarious. But on no account should any attempt be made to haul them to the top of the cliff until the arrival of the coastguards or fishermen with ropes of proven strength.

Various parts of the coast possess dangers peculiar to that particular district, and the summer visitor would be well advised to make himself acquainted with these at the commencement of his holiday. The cliff-tops of Western Cornwall, for instance, are pitted with the shafts of countless old tin mines, many of them unmarked and unfenced, and concealed by rampant growths of heather and bracken. Hundreds of other dangerous workings are merely surrounded by low stone walls, barely three feet high, such as unsuspecting children would delight in jumping over.

These derelict mine shafts present prospects of a truly terrible death. Many of them are hundreds of feet deep and flooded with water, and according to various authorities in the county they are estimated to claim thousands of horses, cattle, dogs and wild creatures every year. As for the number of human beings they have swallowed, the figures will never be known, although they almost certainly run into hundreds. Many a lone walker of the moorland cliff-tops must have disappeared headlong into one of these death-traps, never to be heard of again. Others, walking in company, are sometimes lucky enough to be rescued alive. Not so very long ago a man who had a hair-raising experience of this sort escaped serious injury, but was nearly asphyxiated by the nauseating gases rising from the decomposing corpses of animals that had tumbled into the shaft before him.

Competing with the horrors of abandoned mine workings are those of mud-banks and quicksands, examples of which are to be found along many stretches of our coasts. Some estuary mud-banks and quicksands are reputed to be capable of swallowing a horse and rider within a couple of minutes, whilst others merely allow a man to sink in up to his waist, and then let him settle no farther. Even these milder forms can be quite terrifying, however; and if no help is at hand they can be dangerous, too, if the victim is trapped in the path of an incoming tide.

Ever since the days of the Ancient Britons, when drowning in quicksands was a capital punishment, this form of death has filled people with a particular horror. In many instances this intense fear of quicksands is the real cause of many seashore tragedies, for it makes the victim panic and struggle, and this in turn hastens his end. It is a point worth stressing, therefore, that quicksands do *not* 'suck down' the people they have trapped. Because the density of wet sand is so very much greater than that of water, it is possible for anybody with sufficient presence of mind to lie on his back and 'float' on the surface of the sand until help arrives.

Although we have now discussed many of the more common dangers to be encountered on or near the seashore, we have by no means exhausted the subject. To do that would require, not a single chapter, but a whole book. Enough has been written here, though, to show that practically all seaside mishaps are avoidable if only a little foresight and common sense are used. Of course, sea air will always give rise to high spritis; but the wise person will ensure that those high spirits do not get out of hand and grow into recklessness that can all too easily lead to tragedy.

FISHING: TACKLE AND TECHNIQUES 21

PIER AND JETTY FISHING

For the novice sea angler who has not yet learnt the knack of casting out from a beach with rod and reel, a pier provides a convenient vantage point for getting the baited tackle into reasonably deep water. Similarly, many anglers who suffer from sea-sickness find that pier fishing provides a welcome compromise between going afloat and remaining shorebound.

It must be stressed, however, that the nature of pier fishing imposes certain limitations on the type of tackle which may be used. For example, the crowded conditions prevailing on many holiday resort piers make it unwise to use a long rod —one about 8 ft. in length will usually be found most convenient, The rod should be powerful enough to lift the *average* fish out of the water, or to steer it clear of underwater piles and girders.

However, when fishing from a tall pier that is likely to yield the occasional heavy fish, such as a large cod or bass, it is advisable to equip oneself with a drop-net. This is simply a bag-shaped net attached to an iron hoop, which can be lowered on a rope to lift the fish out of the water—thus avoiding unnecessary strain on one's rod and line.

The two methods most commonly used from a pier are bottom fishing and float fishing.

When bottom fishing, the terminal tackle (i.e. the 'trace' attached to the end of the reel line) can take a multiplicity of forms. However, the types known as paternoster, paternoster-trot and leger will meet most requirements, and the accompanying drawings will explain their nature better than any words. They can be made up very quickly and cheaply from a spool of nylon monofilament, but when doing so it is most important to use the correct knots described later in this book.

In the case of the leger arrangement, it will be noted that

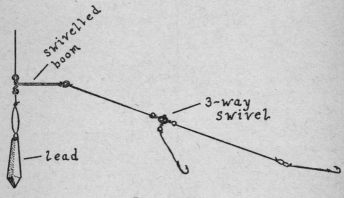

Paternoster-trot

the pull of a biting fish is transmitted direct to the rod-tip *through* the sliding lead. The resistance of a fixed lead, on the other hand, would quickly arouse the suspicions of a fish, and at the same time would prevent the bite being felt properly by the angler.

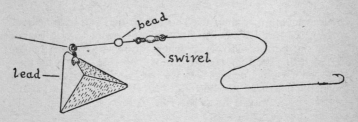

Leger tackle, with swivelled pyramid-shaped lead sliding freely on the reel line

203

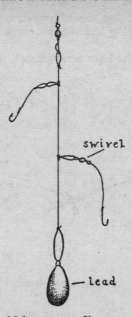

Nylon monofilament paternoster. (NOTE: Hook snoods are attached to paternoster dropper loops tied in the nylon trace.)

Float tackle is mainly used to catch such fish as mackerel, garfish, scad and bass, which frequently swim some distance above the bottom. However, when the sea-bed is too snaggy to risk using bottom tackle, a float can sometimes be used to catch species such as pollack, wrasse and bream, which normally live near the bottom. The elevated position of the angler on the pier reduces the risk of the fish gaining refuge among the sea-bed rocks.

Because of the considerable depth of water usually involved, a fixed float would jam against the tip of the rod when reeling in, leaving the fish still dangling out of reach. So it is customary in sea angling to use a sliding float which slips down the line as the line is retrieved (see illustration).

After casting out this type of sliding float tackle, the lead and baited hook sink downwards, causing the float to slide

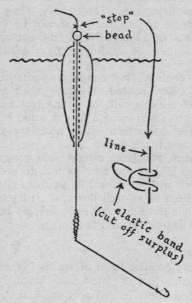

Sliding float tackle

up the line until checked by a 'stop' made from a piece of elastic band. By moving this stop up or down the reel line one can, of course, adjust the fishing depth.

So far we have dealt mainly with fishing from the popular type of pleasure pier, but very often it is possible to obtain better and more enjoyable sport from stone harbour break-waters, and modest little estuary jetties. Not only are they likely to be less crowded, but the angler will usually be fishing closer to the water, with a flight of steps nearby, and so can use much lighter tackle.

For example, it is possible to spin for bass, pollack, mackerel, garfish and coalfish, using a medium spinning rod and fixed-spool reel loaded with about 10 lb. breaking strain nylon monofilament line. For this type of fishing a silvery self-weighted wobbling spoon can be very killing.

(For the benefit of beginners it should be explained that spinning consists of repeatedly casting out and retrieving a small artificial lure, or small dead fish mounted on a spinning flight.)

By way of contrast, big conger are often to be caught when fishing from an old, crevice-pocked harbour wall. These powerful sea-eels call for strong tackle and are most likely to be taken when using a fish or squid bait after dark. As conger have sharp teeth, it is necessary to fit a short length of wire next to the hook.

Similarly, when you have caught your conger, be careful not to put your fingers too near its mouth, and don't try to remove the hook without the aid of a pair of pliers. In fact, if the hook has been taken well down, don't try to remove the hook at all while the fish is alive, but simply unclip the wire trace from the link-swivel, and fit another.

BEACH FISHING

This is a very popular form of sea fishing, and on a good stretch of coast, when conditions are suitable, it can yield some very good sport indeed with such fish as bass, cod, whiting, pouting, conger, dogfish, thornback ray, flatfish and —in some localities—tope.

Needless to say, local shore conditions vary tremendously. On exposed ocean-facing coasts the angler may have to cast far out into heavy surf, using 4 or 6 ounces of lead in order to prevent his bait being flung back by the waves. Such beaches often yield good bass.

By way of contrast, there are sheltered estuaries and sandy bays where only an ounce of lead suffices, and it is possible to cast out ground tackle with a medium spinning rod.

For the general run of open beaches, however, it is customary to use a reasonably powerful rod, about 10 to 11 feet in length, and capable of casting 4 to 6 ounces of lead. Because of its lightness, and ability to stand up to hard use and repeated wetting with salt water, tubular fibreglass is the most popular material for beachcasting rods today.

A rod of this type needs to be matched with a suitable shorecasting reel—the modern trend being to use a light multiplier, large fixed-spool, or a sidecaster. The formerly

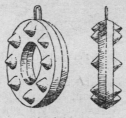

'Grip' lead

popular Nottingham and Scarborough centrepin reels are not used very much by shore anglers nowadays, except on the east coast.

Terminal tackle has also undergone a radical change in recent years, and no longer is it customary to use wire-boomed paternosters and similar 'ironmongery'. Instead, simple home-made nylon monofilament traces are favoured.

BOAT FISHING

There are many different forms of boat fishing, ranging from dinghy angling in a sheltered tidal estuary to deep-sea fishing in large craft up to 10 miles or more from harbour. To a large degree the tackle and methods one uses will depend upon such factors as the depth of water, species of fish being sought, the size of boat being used, and the strength of the tidal currents.

Inshore fishing in a dinghy or small motor boat is capable of providing first-class sport in an estuary, or on a stretch of coast that is reasonably sheltered and free from dangerous tide-races. All the methods suggested for pier fishing can be used when the boat is anchored; or, alternatively, an artificial lure or natural bait can be trolled behind the boat while it is kept on the move with oars, motor or sail.

3-hook mackerel spinner, by Allcocks

Mackerel, pollack, bass and coalfish are commonly taken in this way; although the bait, fishing depth and speed of the boat will have to be varied slightly to suit each species.

Mackerel, for example, are likely to be found almost anywhere and at any depth, provided the water is not too 'cloudy' with stirred-up mud or sand. Pollack and coalfish are encountered mainly over reefs, and swim fairly deep except around dawn or evening, when they tend to swim at higher levels. Bass are found mostly near river estuaries, inshore reefs and sand-bars.

Jardine spiral lead

Driftlining at anchor is another rewarding method commonly used by the inshore boat angler. The line, carrying a single baited hook on a flowing trace, and just enough lead to overcome the pressure of the tide, is drifted down astern until the bait reaches the desired fishing depth. It is a particularly good method for bass when using a live prawn, sandeel or peeler crab bait.

Opinions vary as to the best tackle outfit for inshore boat fishing, but certainly for dinghy work the rod should be kept reasonably short—say somewhere between 6 feet and 7½ feet. Fibreglass, without any doubt, is the most serviceable rod material for boat fishing, and my own preference lies with the 'one-piece' type of rod—i.e. a 2-ft. wooden butt with screw reel fitting, and a single tip section about 4 to 5 feet in length. Such a rod would also be suitable for the lighter kinds of deep-sea fishing; whilst the same butt could be fitted with an alternative heavy-duty tip when after such species as big conger, skate and shark.

Reels for boat fishing should be sturdy, possess an adequate line capacity, and be fitted with an optional check. The two most popular types are the single-action centrepin, and the multiplier. Shark fishing calls for a reel fitted with a slipping clutch and non-reverse handles, if broken fingers are to be avoided.

HOOKS

Sea hooks are made in hundreds of different shapes and sizes, and most beginners find themselves sorely perplexed when it comes to making a choice from such a large range. Fortunately hooks are very cheap, and for a few shillings

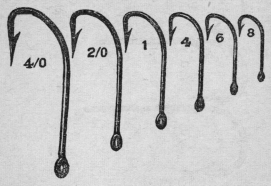

Selection of 'Limerick' hooks

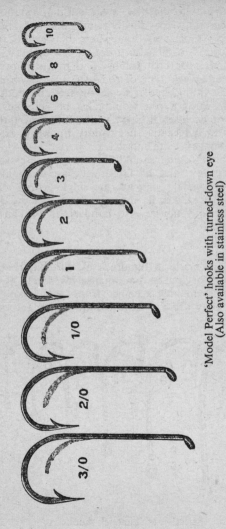

'Model Perfect' hooks with turned-down eye
(Also available in stainless steel)

it is possible to obtain a selection of the most useful sizes, ranging from about 5/0 down to size 6 for the general run of shore and inshore boat fishing. For specialist tope and conger fishing one would need some larger hooks—say 8/0, 7/0 and 6/0.

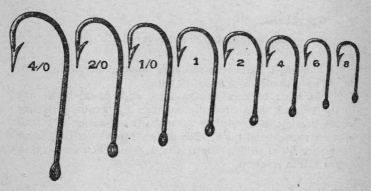

Selection of 'Kirby' hooks

Turned-down eyed 'Kirby' hook (long-shank) with 6 inches of nylon knotted at the loop

Conger eel hook with swivel at end of shank

On the other hand, for specialist grey mullet fishing one would need smaller size 8 and 10 hooks.

Hooks must be kept needle-sharp, and should be as fine in the wire as their strength requirements permit. It is also worth bearing in mind that worm baits are easier to thread on to a round-bend hook, such as the 'Model Perfect'. Some hooks are fitted with a 'sliced' shank, which helps to keep a worm bait in position.

SUNDRIES

Apart from the rod, reel, line, traces and hooks already mentioned, the following additional items will be required for most branches of sea angling:

Tackle box or haversack.

Selection of lead weights.

Spare brass swivels and swivel-links, in various sizes for threadline spinning, shore fishing and deep-sea work.

Spools of nylon monofilament for making up spare traces.

Small tin containing elastic bands and plastic beads for use when legering or float fishing.

Pair of long-nosed pliers for removing hooks, making up wire traces, etc.

Sharp knife for cutting up baits.

Small Carborundum slip for sharpening hooks and knife.

A strong gaff. (Or, alternatively, a landing net when fishing light for mullet, etc.)

Bait box. (Better than a tin, which will quickly corrode and hasten the death of live baits.)

One of the first things the novice at sea fishing should do is to make himself thoroughly familiar with those knots used for tying nylon to nylon, nylon to hooks, wire to hooks, and line to swivels, etc. Not only will this save time in the long run, but will also prevent the loss of tackle and fish through unorthodox knots parting under strain. The knots illustrated here are the ones most commonly used by sea anglers when using modern nylon and terylene lines.

Blood knot. For joining two ends of line.

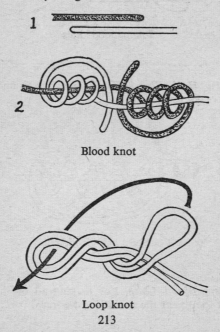

Blood knot

Loop knot

Loop Knot. For making a loop at the end of one's line or trace.

Joining Loop Knots. By making loop ends to one's tackle it is possible to avoid wasting time on the fishing grounds through having to tie knots with wet fingers. Loop ends are especially useful for attaching hook snoods to the trace, for by this means it is possible to change hooks in a matter of seconds.

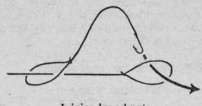

Joining loop knots

Four-Turn Half Blood Knot. For attaching line to a swivel-eye, or straight-eyed hook.

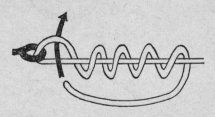

Four-turn half-blood knot

Paternoster Blood Loop. For making an out-jutting hook attachment loop near the middle of the trace.

214

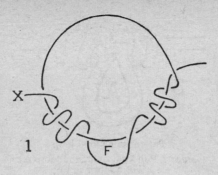

Paternoster blood loop

Stage 1. Make a circle in the line
where you wish to tie the loop.
Twist end X round the circle three
times. Then place a finger at point F
between X and the circle of line, and
twist end X around the circle another
three times

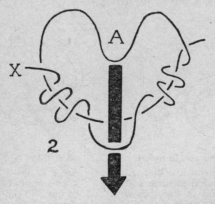

Paternoster blood loop

Stage 2. Withdraw finger from point
F so as to form a gap in the twists,
and at the same time pull the top
part of the circle (A) through the gap

215

Paternoster blood loop
Stage 3. Pull knot tight, and loop (A)
will be formed

Attaching Hook to Nylon. The two-circle turle knot,
illustrated here, is a strong knot suitable for hooks with a
turned-down or turned-up eye.

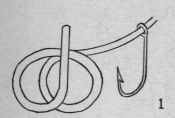

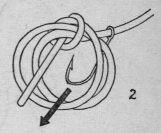

Attaching hook to nylon

Stage 1. Thread line through
hook-eye and then form two
circles at end of line, below
the hook

Attaching hook to nylon

Stage 2. Tie a simple slip
knot around the two circles
of line and pull it tight, as
shown. Thrust the hook
through the circles, as
indicated by the arrow,
and finally tighten the knot
around the hook-shank,
immediately below the eye

Attaching Hook to Wire. Some kinds of *limp* twisted stainless wire can be knotted as shown here. The 'tag-end' is best cut short and covered with Araldite. Other stiffer kinds of wire must be attached to hooks and swivels with a special crimping tool.

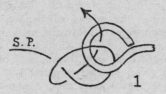

Attaching hook to wire (Stage 1). NOTE: S.P. represents the 'standing part' of the knot

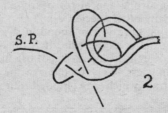

Attaching hook to wire (Stage 2)

This chapter gives details of the sea-fishing baits most commonly used around the coasts of Britain. Some of them, such as the lugworm and ragworm, may often be bought from local tackle dealers. For the benefit of those anglers preferring to gather their own, however, a description of the various baits is given below; together with some information about the places where they are most likely to be found. Although these baits do not interest all species of fish to the same degree, no attempt has been made here to classify their 'appeal value'. This aspect is dealt with fully in the next chapter.

Lugworm. This is one of the most universal baits, and, when fresh, has a strong appeal for nearly all bottom feeding fish, as well as many other species.

The lug is a longshore worm, found in stretches of muddy sand exposed by the receding tide. It is obtained by digging —a garden fork usually being easier to use in the damp sand than a spade, and less likely to damage the worms. In any case, those worms which are injured during the digging

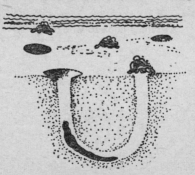

Lugworm burrowing

218

process should be placed in a separate bait box, and used before the sound ones.

The secret of finding them is to look for the tell-tale 'casts' and small crater-like depressions in the sand, caused by the worm's presence immediately below the surface. When sufficient worms have been collected, a small quantity of damp sand should be placed in the bait box to help keep them alive. Care should be taken to protect them from direct sunshine or rain, as both will quickly prove fatal to the worms. The contents of the box should be inspected periodically, and any dead worms removed.

Ragworm. This is another excellent worm bait, found in

Ragworm

the mud, or mixed shingle and mud, of river estuaries.

Ragworms are flattish in shape ; the body having a fringe of legs on either side, and the head being armed with a pair of hooked nippers. These latter are capable of giving the person who handles them carelessly quite a sharp prick, and to avoid this happening the worm should be held firmly behind the head when placing it on the hook. Methods of baiting ragworm vary, but one of the best ways is to insert the point of the hook in the mouth, bringing it out again as far down the body as possible. After that the worm should be doubled over and placed on the hook again. If some of the worm is left dangling from the hook it will prove all the more attractive to the fish.

Ragworms are more hardy than lugworms, and may be kept alive in the bait box for several days if placed between layers of clean sacking that has previously been washed in sea water, and then wrung almost dry again. The contents of the box should be inspected daily, and any dead worms removed immediately.

King Ragworm. This is the name given to a larger species of ragworm, often attaining a length of more than seven inches. It has a tough skin, and in consequence stays on the hook well when casting out from the shore.

Lobworm. In districts where neither lugworms nor ragworms are obtainable, the ordinary garden worm will make a reasonably good bait for estuary flounders. The best worms are the large 'juicy' red ones, generally to be found in manure or compost heaps. They may be kept alive for several days in clean, damp soil, leaf mould, or moss ; care being taken to remove any dead worms at least once every day.

Mussels. An excellent all-round bait, clean to handle, and often obtainable where other baits are scarce. There is a knack in opening the shells, and for this job a knife with a stout, pointed blade is essential.

Mussels are commonly found around the shores of river estuaries, on the rocks bordering sheltered sea lochs, and in large clusters on harbour piles. Their only disadvantage lies in the fact that, being rather a soft bait, they fail to stay on the hook well when casting out from the shore. In consequence, they are best used when boat fishing. For the same reason mussel bait should be inspected at frequent intervals in order to make sure that one is not fishing with bare hooks.

Immersing mussels in hot water for a few seconds will both open their shells and harden the bait, but as the mussel is killed in the process it is doubtful whether it has the same appeal to fish.

Peeler and Soft Crabs. The common greenish-brown shore crab is eaten by many species of fish, including bass. Unfortunately, in its hard-shelled form, this crab does not make a satisfactory hook-bait, and the angler must use crabs which, in the natural process of growing, are moulting their shells.

A crab which is on the point of shedding its shell is known as a 'peeler'. The angler hastens the peeling process by cracking away the old shell ; thus exposing the new shell— which is still soft and fleshy to the touch.

220

The softness of this new shell makes it easy for the crab to be placed on the hook. One simple method of doing this is to remove one of the crab's back legs, and then insert the hook-point in the socket. The hook is passed through the body and brought out near the centre of its back. When casting out, it is advisable to secure the crab on the hook by twisting some elasticated thread around the hook-shank, and then passing it several times around the crab's body; finally securing the other end of the thread to the hook shank again.

A crab which has already shed its old shell naturally, and has not yet formed a new hard shell, is known as a 'soft' crab. It can, of course, be placed on the hook in the same way as a peeler.

Soft and peeler crabs are usually found fairly low down on stretches of sheltered shore, where low tides expose weedy rocks mixed with soft mud. Estuaries are often particularly favourable hunting grounds for this type of bait—the crabs usually being found by turning over clumps of bladder-wrack, or possibly the boulders themselves. Very often the crabs are almost hidden from sight in the soft mud.

When you happen upon a large cock crab carrying a smaller hen crab around under his abdomen, the latter will almost certainly be a peeler or soft crab. Pick the big crab up by grasping it across the carapace behind its claws, and it will soon drop the smaller one. Place the hen crab in your bait box, and discard the big cock crab, which will certainly be a useless hardback.

Soft crabs, of course, can be distinguished by prodding their backs with an outstretched finger. Sometimes the carapace will be found to have already started the hardening process, so that it feels crinkly, like thick brown paper. These are often known as 'paper-backs'. They are worth keeping for bait; although they are not so good as the genuine soft or peeler crab.

Crabs being kept for bait are best stored under damp sea-weed in wooden boxes; or, better still, in a floating courge. It is important to keep soft crabs separate from peelers.

Razorfish. These elongated bivalve molluscs are found in

221

flat expanses of sand near the low water mark of spring tides. They make an excellent bass bait, and stay on the hook well when casting.

A razorfish burrow can be recognised by its keyhole-shaped entrance, and the common method of gathering them is to approach this hole as softly as possible, and then pour some salt into it. The salt is then washed into the hole with a jet of sea water from a punctured plastic bag—whereupon the razorfish will rise to the surface and a spade can be slid underneath it.

Razorfish can also be pulled out of their burrows with a special spear, but this tends to damage the flesh, and their keeping qualities. Undamaged razorfish, on the other hand, can be kept alive for some time in a plastic bucket filled with sea water. Also, provided they are alive, they can be deep-frozen without making the flesh unduly soft.

Squid and Cuttle-fish. Sometimes found washed up on the beach, or obtainable from trawler crews. They are excellent bait for conger, bass, pouting, whiting, cod, and many other fish, and being tough possess the advantage of staying on the hook well.

Sandeels. The sandeels generally used as bait are small silvery fish, about five or six inches long, which bury themselves in damp sand. In many places they may be dug out of their hiding-places at low tide with a garden fork or, better still, a tined clod-hoe. They are often used as a live bait, and if being collected for that purpose should be transferred immediately to a vessel containing sea water—preferably a courge, or lidded container, floating in the sea itself.

Lesser sandeel (nearly life size)

An ordinary metal bucket should not be used, as the action of salt water on galvanised iron quickly kills these delicate fish. If no courge is available they may be kept alive for some time in damp sacking.

When baiting with sandeels, the point of the hook should be thrust in at the mouth and out through the gills; then through the lower part of the body, just behind the head.

Prawns. When used as a live bait, prawns form an excellent lure for those fish which normally haunt rocky stretches of coast, such as pollack, coalfish and bass. In order that the bait may be presented to the fish in as natural a manner as possible, the hook should be passed through the second joint from the tail. Full details concerning the various methods of catching prawns will be found in an earlier chapter of this book.

Mackerel. When fresh, mackerel flesh forms an attractive bait for many fish—including other mackerel. The firm flesh on the side of a mackerel's body, just in front of the tail, is particularly favoured for attaching to the hook of the spinner or driftline. It should be cut with a very sharp knife or razor blade so that it is about $1\frac{1}{4}$ inches long, and half an inch wide, tapering to a point—the skin being half silver and half blue. This type of bait is known as a 'lask' or 'last', and if firmly fixed to the hook will often catch a dozen or more fish before having to be renewed.

Pilchards. An excellent bait, but limited to West Country waters. For best results these fish should be used when fresh, and should, for preference, be bought from the professional fishermen as soon as they return to port.

Herrings. Another excellent fish bait which, like the two mentioned previously, attracts by the natural oil its flesh releases into the water.

The following is a list of fish taken on rod and line in British waters, giving details of their haunts, feeding habits, and the methods commonly used to catch them:

BASS. Found around the south and south-west coasts of Britain, from the Wash to North Wales. Also plentiful around the south coast of Eire. Coloration is bluish-grey on the back, shading to silver underneath. Notable catches weighing up to eighteen pounds have been made with rod and line, but a six-pounder is a good fish by most standards. A great fighter.

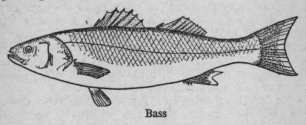

Bass

Habitat. During late spring, summer and autumn good-sized bass are generally to be found in the vicinity of inshore reefs, rocky headlands, sandbars and tidal estuaries.

Food. Bass are voracious feeders, and are particularly partial to prawns, sandeels. sprats, whitebait, shore crabs and young pilchards.

Shore Fishing. (i) Bottom tackle (nylon paternoster or leger) cast out on to snag-free ground from beach, pier or rocky promontory; or into a sandy gully between rocks. (ii) Sliding float tackle from rocks, jetty or pier. (iii) Spinning from rocks, jetty or estuary sand-spit; or from a beach or headland over the top of submerged rocks. (iv) Drift-lining from the end of a pier or jetty.

Boat Fishing. (i) Spinning near shoaling bass, or in likely feeding areas, from a drifting dinghy. (ii) Trolling with a live sandeel or artificial lure. (iii) Driftlining from an anchored boat. (iv) Sliding float gear baited with live prawn or ragworm, and fished in a shallow rocky cove. (v) Drifting close to rocks in a dinghy, trailing a live prawn on un-weighted tackle.

Baits. Sandeels and prawns (preferably live) ; peeler and soft crab ; lugworm, ragworm, strips of squid, mackerel and herring lures. Long, narrow silver wobbling spoons ; plastic Mevagissey sandeel ; rubber eel ; German sprat, etc.

BREAM. Two species of sea bream inhabit British waters, the Red Bream and the Black Bream. The latter is a some-what localised fish, being caught on the south coast mostly around Littlehampton and Bognor Regis, and parts of Hampshire, the Isle of Wight and Dorset. The Red Bream, although less common than it was years ago, is still caught in fair numbers off south-west England and parts of Ireland. As its name implies, it is of a reddish tinge ; brownish-scarlet on the back, shading to reddish-silver on the sides and belly. Adult fish have a dark patch on the shoulder. The younger fish, which lack this patch, are known as chad.

From April to August bream appear off the south coast in small shoals, seldom venturing very far north as they prefer warm water. They make excellent eating when grilled or baked.

Habitat. Both red and black bream favour areas of weedy rock or rough ground, and are usually (but not always) found fairly near the bottom.

Food. The bream has a rather small mouth, and it lives mainly on shrimps, brittle stars, worms and small bivalves.

Shore Fishing. Only practicable in a few favoured places, using a light nylon paternoster or paternoster-trot. Also by deep driftlining or float fishing from a pier or harbour break-water.

Boat Fishing. Light 7 lb. driftline trace and size 6 hook, fished with a light and lively rod, and a centrepin reel loaded

H   225

with about 9 lb. nylon monofilament line. NOTE. Catches are improved by groundbaiting with crushed crabs, or a mixture of bran and cod liver oil, suspended below the boat in a sack or net bag.

Baits. Narrow strips of mackerel or herring; lug, ragworm, mussel.

COALFISH and POLLAK. These two fish are very similar in their appearance and habits, and can be caught by similar methods. The coalfish is darker coloured, being bluish-black on the back, shading to silvery below. The pollack is dark greenish-bronze on the back, shading to bronze and silver on the sides and belly. With certain exceptions and 'overlapping', the coalfish is found mostly in our northern waters; whereas the pollack is mainly encountered along the southern and western coasts.

Habitat. Usually found over or near rocks, and around rocky headlands. Mostly swims near the bottom, but rises to other levels when hunting—particularly around dawn and evening.

Food. Adult coalfish and pollack prey largely upon other fish. The smaller ones feed on sandeels, small fry, prawns, shrimps, etc.

Shore Fishing. (i) Spinning from, or close to, rocky headlands, reefs, stone harbour walls, etc. (ii) Float fishing from similar vantage points.

Boat Fishing. (i) Spinning. (ii) Trolling with rubber eel. (iii) Feathering.

Baits. Ragworm, sandeel (preferably live), peeler crab, strips of mackerel, pilchard.

Lures. Rubber eel, plastic sandeel, silver wobbling spoon, feathered jigs, etc.

COD. Encountered in British inshore waters mainly during the autumn and winter months. The best cod fishing is to be had around our northern, eastern and south-eastern (especially Kent) coasts. Small cod to about 6 lb. are generally referred to as codling.

Habitat. A bottom-feeder, favouring sandy or broken ground; also areas of kelp and rock on some coasts.

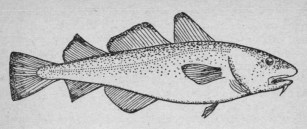

Cod

Food. Preys on a wide variety of marine creatures, including smaller fish, shrimps, prawns, cuttlefish and worms.

Shore Fishing. Bottom tackle (nylon paternoster or leger) from steep-to beach or pier.

Boat Fishing. Paternoster, paternoster-trot or driftline fished on or just tripping above the bottom.

Baits. Lugworms, mussels, peeler crab, mackerel and herring strips, etc.

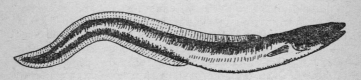

Conger Eel

CONGER. The novice at sea fishing contemplates catching his first big conger eel with mixed feelings. To bag one of these monsters of the deep would, he feels, be something to brag about afterwards. On the other hand, there is something about the appearance of a large conger that makes otherwise stout-hearted men think twice about having any close dealings with these creatures. The female conger may attain a length up to seven or eight feet, possesses a body as thick as a big man's thigh, and has a wicked-looking, serpent-like head filled with teeth that are quite capable of removing the thumb of a careless angler. In view of these

227

facts, there may be some who will decide that they have no particular desire to catch a conger. However, they had better read on and learn how to cope with them, as congers are notoriously obstinate brutes, and on many parts of the coast simply insist on being caught!

Habitat. Lives on the bottom amongst crevice-filled rocks, sunken wrecks and underwater caverns.

Food. Preys on other fish.

Shore Fishing. Leger tackle cast out on snag-free ground close to rocks, or a sea-eroded stone harbour wall.

Boat Fishing. Leger tackle streamed down to a suitable rock mark or sunken wreck. NOTE. Owing to the conger's sharp teeth it is essential to fit a few inches of flexible cable-laid stainless wire next to the hook.

Baits. Large strips of herring, mackerel, squid; small whole pouting or whiting.

Note. A conger is best gaffed near the head, and it can be quietened by hitting it in the region of the vent with the proverbial 'blunt instrument'. However, do not attempt to remove the hook from its mouth until you are certain that it is quite dead. If you wish to continue your fishing, remove the hook from your tackle and fit another one. To facilitate this operation the wire trace of the conger hook should have been attached to the tackle with a combined swivel and clip, obtainable from any tackle dealer for a few pence.

Finally, when bringing your catch ashore, keep inquisitive children away from it. More than one angler has filled the role of defendant in an expensive lawsuit because some child's prodding finger has been badly bitten by an apparently lifeless conger while its captor's back was turned.

DAB. This tasty little flatfish is found all round the British Isles.

Habitat. Areas of fine sand or muddy sand.

Food. Mainly marine worms, starfish, bivalves, etc.

Shore and Boat Fishing. Light nylon paternoster or leger, fitted with small hooks—say about size 6 to 8, depending on bait used.

Baits. Ragworm, lug, mussel, razorfish, peeled shrimp.

DOGFISH, LESSER and GREATER SPOTTED. These two species

of dogfish give little sport, but make good eating when one has learnt the knack of skinning them. They are a plague on most coasts, and are taken on various kinds of bottom tackle when using fish strips, lugworm, etc. The Lesser Spotted dogfish favours sandy ground; whereas the Greater Spotted species (also known as 'bull huss') are usually found near rock.

DOGFISH, SPUR. Mainly caught when fishing for other species—notably whiting, upon which it preys. In appearance it resembles a small greyish-coloured tope. Beware of its two venomous spurs, situated in front of its dorsal fins.

FLOUNDER. These medium-sized flatfish are usually found in river estuaries where the bottom is sand or mud.

Food. Shore crabs, sandeels, lugworms, shrimps and small fry.

Shore Fishing. (i) Light nylon paternoster or leger. (ii) Spinning with a baited-spoon.

Boat Fishing. (i) Light nylon paternoster or leger. (ii) Trolling with a baited-spoon.

Baits. Ragworm and lug (baited-spoon and bottom fishing); peeler crab (bottom).

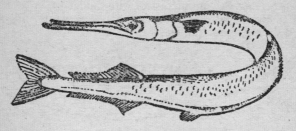

Garfish or needlefish

GARFISH. A most unusual looking fish, possessing a beaked mouth that has caused it to be known as the Longnose along the Dorset coast. This beak makes it rather difficult to hook; although it is quite often taken when spinning or trolling with small mackerel lures. It is also frequently caught on light float tackle intended for mackerel, pollack, etc.

229

When hooked it often leaps clear of the water in spectacular fashion, and in doing so not infrequently rids itself of the hook.

Garfish are useful as bait, and the author once caught a 24½ lb. turbot when baiting with a garfish tail.

GREY MULLET. Often very numerous in river estuaries and creeks. Also common in harbours, where they feed on galley scraps and offal cast overboard from fishing boats. As a rule these harbour mullet are more easily caught than the very shy and wary creek mullet.

Food. Very varied, and includes many tiny marine creatures.

Shore Fishing. Mullet are taken from piers, harbour walls, estuary revetments, etc. Groundbaiting little and often is usually essential for success, but at some favourite mulleting spots this is done for the angler through scraps of food being washed out from factory wastepipes, harbour fish-gutting sheds, pier cafés, etc. Light float tackle is a favourite method, using size 8 or 10 hooks.

Mullet may also be caught by spinning with a tiny ragworm-baited fly spoon.

Boat Fishing. Seldom successful with mullet.

Baits. Bread paste or flake, small red ragworm, maggots, peeled shrimp, bacon fat, etc.

Mackerel

MACKEREL. This handsome streamlined fish is found all round the British Isles during the summer months. For its size, it is the most powerful of our sea fish, and gives grand sport on light tackle.

Habitat. Nomadic.

Food. Early-season mackerel are largely plankton feeders

—but gradually they turn their attention to larger forms of food, such as whitebait, sandeels, sprats, etc.

Shore Fishing. (i) Threadline spinning with a small silvery lure. (ii) Heavy spinning with a feathered trace. (iii) Light float fishing.

Boat Fishing. (i) Threadline spinning from a drifting boat; (ii) Trolling with a mackerel spinner. (iii) Light float fishing. (iv) Feathering—a non-sporting method used mainly by rod anglers as a quick method of catching bait.

Baits. Mackerel slips, sandeels (preferably live).

Lures. Silver spoons, German sprat, plastic sandeel, feathered trace, or single feathered lure.

PLAICE. These familiar flatfish are to be found around most parts of the coast where the sea-bed is of firm sand, shell-grit or muddy sand.

Food. Marine worms, burrowing molluscs and shrimps.

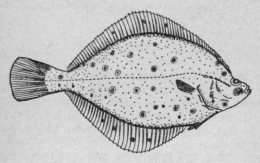

Plaice

Shore and Boat Fishing. Bottom fishing with a light nylon paternoster-trot or leger.

Baits. Ragworm, razorfish, lugworm, cockle, mussel.

POUTING. Lives on broken and rocky areas of sea-bed, and is particularly common around south-western coasts—although it may be encountered elsewhere.

Food. Small shore and swimming crabs, marine worms, prawns, etc.

231

Shore Fishing. Nylon leger or paternoster carrying a size 4 to 6 hook.

Boat Fishing. A driftline or paternoster fished about 1 to 3 ft. above rough ground, and carrying a size 1/0 (deep-sea) to size 4 (inshore) hook.

Baits. Mackerel, herring or squid strips, ragworm, lug, prawns, mussels, shelled garden snails.

SHAD, TWAITE. This slender but deep-bodied silvery fish is related to the herring, and is the species of shad most likely to be taken on rod and line in British waters. There is often a row of dark spots along the upper sides of its body.

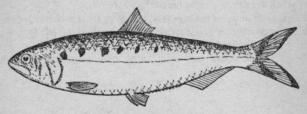

Twaite shad

In summer and early autumn it is present around many parts of the coast, from the English Channel to Scotland, but is most likely to be encountered in the vicinity of estuaries. It is sometimes taken when feathering or trolling for mackerel, and also on light float tackle baited with small harbour ragworm.

In April, May and June large shoals of twaite shad enter rivers to spawn in the upper tidal reaches, and in some areas they provide excellent sport for 'freshwater' anglers using tiny spinners, or (in some places) flies.

This fish makes pleasant eating, although the numerous small bones are a nuisance.

SHARK. Four species of shark are taken on rod and line in British and Irish waters—the blue shark (the most common species), the porbeagle, the mako, and the thresher. Shark fishing calls for specialist tackle and methods, and space limitations prevent us from going into lengthy details here.

The beginner would be well advised to visit one of the recognised shark fishing centres, which include Looe, Torquay, Falmouth, Fowey, Mevagissey and Penzance in the West Country; and Kinsale, Cobh and Ballycotton in Ireland. At most of these places it is possible to hire suitable tackle.

SKATE, COMMON. These large 'winged' fish are caught mostly by deep-sea anglers fishing several miles offshore; although in parts of Ireland (notably in Cobh Harbour) huge specimens weighing up to 170 lb. are frequently taken quite close to land. Rod, reel and line have to be strong, and the terminal tackle usually consists of a strong leger with wire next to a forged 8/0 hook baited with a whole fillet of mackerel. For this type of fishing the angler must wear a padded 'tarpon belt' to protect himself from being injured by pressure from the rod butt.

SOLE. These oval-shaped flatfish are rather localised, and are caught mostly around the southern half of the British Isles. They come inshore during the summer months.

Habitat. Areas of soft sand or mud—often with scattered rocks.

Food. Marine worms, starfish, shrimps and burrowing molluscs.

Shore and Boat Fishing. Light nylon leger or paternoster-trot baited with ragworm or lugworm.

THORNBACK RAY. This small member of the skate tribe

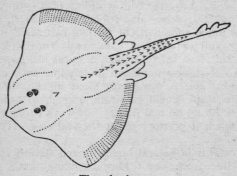

Thornback ray

averages about 10 lb., and rarely exceeds 17 to 20 lb. It is often found close inshore. The wings make excellent eating.

Habitat. Sandy and gravelly areas of sea-bed, including some estuaries.

Food. Shrimps, small flatfish, small crabs, etc.

Shore Fishing. Possibly from a few favoured piers and beaches, using leger tackle and a 4/0 hook.

Boat Fishing. Leger tackle.

Baits. Strips of mackerel or herring; peeler crab, prawns.

TOPE. This small member of the shark family is found around the south-eastern, southern and western coasts of England and Wales; and is also numerous around southern and western Ireland.

Habitat. Nomadic, but usually found near the bottom in sandy areas, or where sand fringes rock. During summer and early autumn it is encountered close inshore.

Food. Preys on other fish.

Shore Fishing. At a few favoured steeply-shelving beaches and rock stations it is possible to catch tope on leger tackle carrying a swivelled 4 ft. plastic-covered wire trace, and forged hook baited with mackerel or herring. Some anglers favour a whole fish; others prefer to use a fillet. A medium shorecasting rod will prove adequate for tope fishing, and there is no need for the line to be heavier than 25 to 30 lb. breaking strain—provided there is plenty of it.

Boat Fishing. Legering with a sliding lead 'stopped' with a piece of matchstick or valve rubber about 20 ft. above the trace. The trace should be of flexible cable-laid wire about 7 ft. long, and swivelled at either end. The hook (to wire) is best attached to the trace with a spiral locking connector, so that if necessary a hook can be left in a tope after it has been caught, and a new hook fitted quickly in its place. NOTE. The 'stop' should be strong enough to hold the lead in position during normal fishing, but weak enough to release the lead when it presses against the end ring of the rod on reeling in.

TURBOT. This large and highly prized flatfish is taken on rod and line from about May to mid-autumn, mostly in favoured areas around the southern half of Britain and

Turbot

Ireland. Fish in the 15 to 20 lb. range are quite common, and it has been caught on rod and line to a weight of 29 lb. (Coverack, 1964).

Habitat. Often found on the edge of steep-to submerged banks of shell-grit or fine sand—particularly in areas where tides run fast.

Food. Feeds on or close to the sea-bed on sandeels and other small fish.

Shore Fishing. A few turbot are caught from favoured piers and beaches every year, but they are taken by chance while bottom fishing for other species.

Boat Fishing. Leger tackle fished either at anchor or on the drift. The turbot has a big mouth, so use a 5/0 or 6/0 hook. Tackle of at least medium strength will be required when fishing at anchor in a fast-running tide.

Baits. Fillet cut from the side of a freshly caught 'cock launce' (greater sandeel); large strip of mackerel or garfish; live poor-cod.

WHITING. These fish spend much of their time in shoals just above areas of sand, muddy sand or shell-grit. During summer months whiting keep mainly to deep water, but the shoals move close inshore in autumn and winter.

Food. Preys on smaller fish, shrimps and small crabs.

Shore Fishing. In late autumn and winter it is possible to take good catches of whiting by casting out bottom tackle (light nylon leger or paternoster) from suitable piers, beaches, etc.

Boat Fishing. Deep-sea in summer ; inshore in winter. (i) Boomed paternoster, usually fished a foot or two above the bottom—although sometimes the fish are found higher in the water. This method can be used either anchored or drifting. (ii) Driftlining from an anchored boat.

Baits. Lugworm, ragworm, mussels ; small strips of herring, mackerel or other whiting ; sprats.

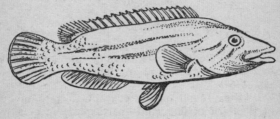

Wrasse

WRASSE. Several species of wrasse inhabit British waters, but the two most commonly caught on rod and line are the Ballan Wrasse and the Cuckoo Wrasse. The latter is very colourful, and somewhat localised, and is mostly encountered around southern and south-western coasts.

Habitat. Reefs, areas of weedy ground, and sunken wrecks. Wrasse move inshore during the summer months.

Food. Small crabs, prawns and molluscs.

Shore Fishing. (i) Bottom fishing on patches of sand close alongside a rocky promontory or reef. This method usually takes the largest fish. (ii) Sliding float tackle fished over rocks.

Boat Fishing. Driftlining or paternostering at anchor over rocky ground.

Baits. Ragworm, prawns, cockle, mussel, peeler crab.

236

So far in this book we have discussed the art of fishing solely from the point of view of the amateur in search of pleasure and recreation. There is, however, no reason at all why fishing for pleasure should not also show a profit; especially if one is fortunate enough to own a boat. In this chapter, therefore, it is proposed to detail a few of the longshore fishing methods available to the person who wishes to catch fish, lobsters, crabs, etc., in larger numbers than is normally possible by those methods commonly employed by amateurs.

Fishmongers in coastal towns are nearly always willing to buy saleable fish offered fresh from the sea; while in smaller places, where there are no fish shops, there is usually a ready market among the local hotels and boarding houses. Of course, on a purely spare-time basis such fishing is unlikely to show a very large profit, but over a season or two it can easily cover the cost of both boat and tackle—*and* leave enough over to treat oneself to a well-earned pint of beer on coming ashore!

Lobster Pots

Lobstering with pots is by no means the prerogative of professional fishermen, and there are plenty of dinghy owners living on suitable stretches of coast who make a practice of setting one or more pots throughout the summer months in order to supply their own table. In the happy event of a catch being made 'surplus to requirements' there is never any difficulty in coming to a profitable arrangement with one of those catering establishments specialising in lobster teas.

Lobster pots are easy enough to make, and if judicious use is made of driftwood and other odds and ends washed up on the beach they will cost practically nothing. The simplest type of pot consists of an oblong, box-shaped wooden framework, completely covered over with twine netting, save for a funnel-shaped entrance at one end. This funnel is usually inclined obliquely upwards so that the lobster is able to crawl into the trap quite easily, but is baffled when it tries to get out again. The trap is, of course,

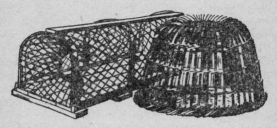

Two types of lobster pot

baited with fish offal, and weighted with concrete to make it sink readily. To the top of the pot is attached a light rope, long enough to reach from the sea bed to the surface at any state of the tide, and buoyed at 12 ft. intervals by a series of corks. It is a good idea to mark the end cork in a distinctive manner with paint in order to make it easy to recognise one's own pot.

Lobster pots vary considerably from district to district. Some localities favour an entrance at either end of the pot to double the chance of a lobster finding a way in; others place the entrance on top, in the belief that this makes it more difficult for the lobster to escape once it has been caught. In Cornwall and South Devon the old-fashioned lobster creel, fashioned out of withies, is still used. Elsewhere, instead of twine netting, wooden slats are nailed across the sides of the frame about an inch apart. Some even use wire netting instead of the twine netting, but most professional fishermen declare that this material does not feel natural to the lobster when it tests it with its claws, and that in consequence the more wary ones will have nothing to do with such traps. Another disadvantage of wire netting is that it quickly rusts away in salt water, and, lacking the resilience of twine netting, is very liable to get broken against jagged rocks.

As lobsters favour a rocky sea bed, pots are placed close to a submerged reef, or off a boulder-strewn headland; usually at depths ranging from two to ten fathoms. Weather permitting, the pots are inspected at least once every day. In rough weather pots in shallow water are frequently shifted considerable distances by the undercurrents, or else become smashed against, or jammed amongst, the rocks. It is always advisable, therefore, to take lobster pots into deeper water whenever a gale warning is broadcast on the radio.

Other things besides lobsters are often found in the pots, such as crabs of various kinds, fish, large prawns and conger eels. Those of value as human food will, of course, be taken back to the shore, but even the inedible part of the catch is often of use, being cut up on the spot and replaced in the pot as bait. There are several favoured methods of baiting a lobster pot, but whichever one is used, the bait should be fixed in such a position that the lobster is bound to enter the pot before it can get its claws on the bait. One efficient method consists of impaling the bait on a long wooden skewer thrust through the sides of the pot and the wicker entrance funnel. Lobsters find the bait mainly by their sense of smell, so it enhances the chance of a catch if the pot is placed in an under-current, as this helps to spread the smell of the bait over a wide area.

A lobster should be removed from the pot as soon as it is brought to the surface, for it is then that it feels most bewildered, and is most easily handled. Nevertheless, even then the claws need to be treated with respect; especially the large 'crusher' claw, which is capable of making a nasty mess of a person's thumb. Large edible crabs, too, are frequently found in pots laid in deep water, and one should also avoid shaking hands with them. Lobsters can sometimes be persuaded to let go; crabs just grip harder and harder.

When two or more lobsters have been caught it is advisable to tie their claws with string to prevent them from fighting amongst themselves and damaging one another. If the catch is to be marketed it should be taken along to the buyer as quickly as possible, as lobsters are only bought when still alive.

Finally, remember the legal aspects of lobstering, mentioned in a previous chapter of this book. It is an offence to offer for sale any lobster that measures less than nine inches from head-spike to tail-tip, or any female lobster that is 'in berry'. Similarly, crabs which measure less than four and a half inches across the shell should also be returned to the sea.

LONG LINES

The owner of a small boat who wishes to turn his time afloat to good account could scarcely do better than try his luck at long lining, or trot-lining as it is sometimes called. The tackle is inexpensive, and can easily be made up at home from a few shillings.

Briefly, a long line consists of a stout line of considerable length, to which are attached at intervals a number of shorter, finer lines, each carrying a hook at its free end. These short lines are called snoods, and when attaching them to the long line the novice would be well advised to make sure that they are spaced so that they cannot become entangled with one another. Snoods measuring fourteen inches, and spaced at five feet intervals, will prove quite satisfactory for cod, skate, ray, conger and dogfish.

A long line is laid along the sea bed, across the tide, in a position where trawling operations are not carried on. Both ends of the line are anchored to large concrete killicks or grapnels, to which are also attached lines rising to cork buoys floating on the surface. These buoys are usually flagged to make it easier for them to be seen from a distance.

The long lines used by large deep-sea boats sometimes measure eight miles in length, and carry as many as four thousand hooks; but, of course, that sort of tackle is out of the question for the small longshore fisherman. A line carrying only a dozen hooks will prove quite long enough for the beginner to manage by himself. Later on, when a fair degree

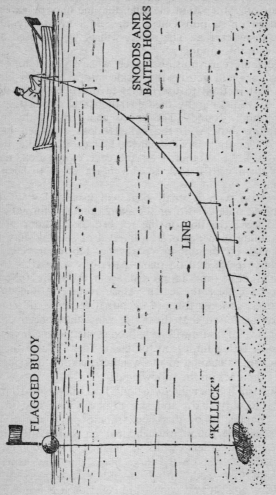

FLAGGED BUOY

SNOODS AND BAITED HOOKS

LINE

"KILLICK"

How to lay and operate a long line

of proficiency has been attained, and tangles have become the exception rather than the rule, the line may be extended by a dozen or so hooks at a time, until eventually about sixty are being carried. The novice will be well advised to be satisfied with this number.

Considerable care must be taken when using a long line if one is to avoid getting the tackle into a hopeless tangle, and the best method to use is that favoured by professional fishermen, who generally bait their hooks before setting out for the fishing grounds. The line is coiled round the inside of a shallow box, with the baited hooks arranged in the centre. A variation of this method is to hang the hooks neatly, one after another, over the edge of the box, finally covering them with a sack soaked in sea water to keep the bait fresh.

The person with a small boat will usually lay his long line within a mile or two or the shore, and the normal practice is to leave the line on the sea bed for an hour or two before hauling it in again. The interval of waiting may then be occupied by handlining, prawning, lobstering, etc. Another system employed on many parts of the coast is to lay the line at dusk, and to go out again early the following morning to collect the catch. This second method brings good results, as most fish are nocturnal feeders; although it will often be found that those fish which have been on the hook for several hours will have been spoiled through congers and dogfish biting lumps out of them. There is also the risk of an overnight change in the weather making it impossible to collect the lines on the following day.

The sort of fish caught on a long line will depend largely upon the locality, bait, and size of the hooks, and in this respect Chapter 24 of this book should prove useful as a guide. It will be found, though, that on the smaller hooks plaice, dabs, flounders, whiting, haddock and codling will predominate; whilst on the large hooks one may expect to catch skate, ray, cod, turbot, dogfish and conger. In districts where dogfish and conger are common it is a good idea to use the type of conger eel hook that incorporates a swivel at the end of the shank. By doing this many bad tangles will be avoided.

GILL NETS

The gill net—or hanging net, as it is called in some parts —is possibly the simplest type of net there is, and in various forms it has been known and used since prehistoric times. It is much favoured by the small fisherman with little capital.

A very fine twine, which nowadays may be made of nylon, is used in the manufacture of a gill net, so that in the water it is practically invisible. Its upper edge is supported at or near the surface by means of cork floats, while the lower edge is weighted with lead sinkers. Thus the net is made to hang perpendicularly, and, as its name implies, the fish become entangled by their gills when attempting to pass through it.

The size of the mesh in a gill net varies according to the type of fish the net is designed to catch. The gauge should be just large enough to allow the passage of the fish's head, yet too small for the body to pass through as well. Herring nets average thirty to thirty-six meshes per yard, pilchard nets thirty-six per yard, and mackerel twenty-five to twenty-nine per yard.

A gill net is anchored across the tide, so that the fish will swim into it as they head into the flow of water. There is rather more to setting a net than that, however; and if one is to obtain good results it will be necessary to study the movements and habits of the fish along a particular stretch of coast. Generally speaking, good places for gill nets are to be found near river estuaries, in the channels formed between an island and the mainland, off headlands, or any place liable to provide food for the fish one is seeking. Thus, when after pollack, it would probably be best to shoot the net just off a rocky headland. It is necessary, though, to keep clear of shipping channels, and those places known to be the haunt of dogfish. Sometimes considerable damage is done to both net and catch by dogfish, and the person who owns a net will have to know how to repair it.

Net braiding is not difficult to learn, and there are also one or two excellent books on the subject that will help to solve any difficulties as they arise. One of the best I have come across is *Nets: how to Make, Mend and Preserve Them*, by G. A. Steven, published in 1950 by Routledge & Kegan Paul Ltd. A word of warning, though, whilst on the subject of books. Treat with suspicion those works of an 'arty-crafty' nature, which tell you how to make shopping bags, and even scarves, out of netting. As a rule the knots depicted in this type of netting manual are quite unsuited to the repair of fishing nets.

SEINE NETS

During the summer months, when mackerel and other sorts of fish venture close inshore in large shoals, considerable catches are often made from the beach with long nets, variously known as seines, seans, or sweep-nets. The upper edge of a seine is rendered buoyant by means of corks, while the lower edge is weighted down with lead sinkers, so that in the water the net hangs vertically, like a curtain. As a rule a seine is much longer than the average gill net, and is a little more complicated in its design as it has a sort of large pouch, known as a 'bunt', midway between the two ends, which in turn are usually referred to as the 'sleeves' or 'wings'. There are several local versions of the seine net, but whichever type is used the underlying principle is the same—the shoal of fish is surrounded by the net and dragged ashore. For obvious reasons, therefore, seining can only be carried on where the beach is free from rocks or other obstructions.

Four men at least are required when seining; or six or more if the net is of any size. They are usually referred to as a 'crew', although not all of them leave the shore. Prior to the commencement of fishing operations the net is carefully loaded into the stern of a fair-sized rowing boat, which is stationed in readiness at the water's edge. A double line, attached to one end of the net, hangs free of the boat, and when an inshore shoal is sighted one member of the fishing crew grabs it and remains on the beach, while the others push out the boat and scramble aboard. With one man in the stern paying out the net as they go, the others row as hard as possible in order to surround the shoal in a wide semi-circle. Returning to the beach at a point some distance from where they started, the crew divides into two equal groups, each hauling in one end of the seine until finally they come to the bunt, in which, if all has gone according to plan, the fish will be gathered in a threshing mass. Quite often a ton or more of mackerel are caught at one 'shooting'. Other fish captured by this method are pilchards, bass, mullet, and an occasional salmon—the latter being hastily hidden from the onlookers who usually crowd around whenever a net is hauled ashore!

Seine nets are expensive nowadays, and professional fisher-men, working as a family group, often make up their own from factory-bought netting as a winter occupation, but it is no job for the beginner. Along some parts of the coast seine fishing is carried on as a spare-time interest in the early mornings and evenings, and at week-ends, by groups of men who share expenses and profits between them. In the long run, taking into account the wear and tear on the net, these crews do not make much money out of their fishing, although they certainly get a lot of fun. A seine needs to be used by a full-time crew, on the beach from dawn to dusk whenever conditions are favourable, if it is to cover its own cost and show a reasonable profit. Such a crew may be seen at work along the Chesil Beach, near Abbotsbury, in Dorset. Their team-work and wonderful sense of timing really is something to watch, and rarely indeed do they miss a shoal.

Seine nets vary in size according to the nature of the beach and the type of fish they are designed to catch. Con-sequently, care should be taken when buying a secondhand net that has seen service on a different beach to that on which one is proposing to use it. On a gently shelving beach, for instance, a seine need only be a few feet deep to per-form its job efficiently, but if that same net were to be used on a steeply shelving beach there would be a gap between the bottom edge of the net and the sea bed, and the shoal would escape. Full-time professional fishermen would never make such an obvious error, of course, but I have known more than one part-time crew waste their money in this way. As for the length of the net, this also varies considerably. Short nets of about 25 yards or so can sometimes be used when working narrow creeks, but a length of 100 yards or more is usually required on open beaches. In America, where they have a habit of doing things in a big way, Seine nets up to 2,000 yards long are in use—the hauling-in operation being performed by tractors, motor-winches, or teams of horses.

GLOSSARY OF NAUTICAL TERMS AND EXPRESSIONS

Abaft: towards the stern of a boat; in the rear of.

Abeam: any point at right-angles to a boat.

Aft: near the stern of a boat.

Amidships: half way between the stem and stern of a ship.

Astern: any point directly behind a boat; to reverse— as in the order: 'Hard astern!'

Backing: a backing wind is one which changes direction 'against the sun'—i.e. from N. and W., through S. to E.

Beam: the widest part of a boat.

Beam Sea: a sea in which the waves or swell approach the boat from the side.

Beams: cross timbers giving support to a deck.

Beamy: description applied to a vessel that is broad in the beam.

Bight: a bay; a loop, or bend, in a rope.

Bilge: the lowest interior part of a vessel's hull; the water collecting there.

Bollard: a squat, pillar-shaped piece of metal or stone on a pier, quay, ship, etc., round which a hawser may be tied or wound.

Bow: the forward end of a boat.

Bowsprit: spar projecting from the bow of a ship.

By the board: fallen overboard.

Carvel-built: a boat so constructed that her planks are laid side by side, giving her a smooth hull.

Caulk: to drive oakum into the seams of a boat.

Cleat: a piece of wood or iron with two projecting arms, round which a rope can be secured.

Clinker-built: a boat so constructed that the planks of her hull overlap.

Cockboat: a small ship's boat.

Cockpit: the undecked part of a small craft from which it is steered.

Counter: the curved, overhanging part of the stern of a vessel.

Fairlead: a piece of metal designed to act as a guide for a rope, and to prevent it rubbing against wooden parts of the boat.

Fathom: six feet.

Flotsam: goods lost at sea which remain floating on the water. (*See* also Jetsam, Ligan and Wreck.)

Following sea: a sea in which the waves approach a boat from stern.

Forecastle, or *Fo'c'sle:* the forward part of a ship below decks, generally used as the crew's quarters.

Foredeck: the deck immediately behind the bows of a boat.

Freeboard: the distance between a boat's gunwales and the waterline.

Gig: a light ship's boat.

Gillick: see Killick.

Gimbals: a contrivance of pivoted rings for keeping lamps, pressure stoves, etc., horizontal at sea.

Gudgeons: metal eyes, usually two in number, fitted to a boat's stern to carry the rudder pintles.

Guy: a rope, or line, used to steady a spar.

Gybe: see Jibe.

Halliard, or *Halyard:* a rope for raising a sail, flag or yard.

Head sea: a sea in which the waves come rolling towards the bow of the boat.

Headway: the forward progress of a boat, as distinct from leeway.

Hitch: a temporary knot, quickly made and untied.

Jetsam: goods cast into the sea which remain under the water. (*See also* Flotsam, Ligan and Wreck.)

Jettison: to cast overboard.

Jibe: to cause the boom of a fore-and-aft sail to swing over suddenly by changing tack with a following wind.

Jury rig: to improvise an item of rigging in order to replace something lost or broken. The replacement is known as a jury mast, jury anchor, jury rudder, etc.

Kedge: a small anchor.

Kedge off: to move a boat by hauling on the anchor cable. This method is often used in order to free a boat that has run aground, the anchor first of all being rowed out into deeper water in the boat's dinghy. Also, it is customary for a sailing craft without auxiliary power to kedge off when an awkward wind is keeping it pinned against a harbour wall, etc.

Keel: the lowest fore-and-aft timber, or steel substitute, on which the hull of a boat is built up.

Killick, or *Gillick:* a large stone used to anchor a small boat when fishing; a large stone used to anchor trot-lines, gill nets, and other fishing tackle.

Knees: angled pieces of wood used to reinforce certain parts of a boat.

Lee shore: a stretch of coast on to which the wind is blowing from the sea.

Lee tide: a tide which has the wind behind it.

Leeward: the side opposite to that on which the wind is blowing.

Leeway: the drift of a boat to leeward.

Lifeline: a safety line, sometimes used when sailing single-handed in rough weather. One end is tied about the waist, and the other end made fast to some part of the boat.

Ligan: goods cast overboard and attached to a buoy for subsequent recovery.

Logline: an apparatus, lowered overboard on the end of a line, used for measuring the speed of a vessel.

Mile, nautical: 6,080 feet. It corresponds to 1/60th of a degree of latitude.

Oakum: loose fibre obtained by unpicking old rope.

Offing: the more distant part of the sea visible to an observer.

Offshore: some fair distance from the shore, but still visible from the land.

Offward: away from the land. For example, a boat setting course out to sea might be described as 'heading offward'.

Painter: the rope used for tying up a small boat to a jetty, etc.

Parcel: to cover a rope with canvas or soft leather to prevent chafing.

Pay: to pitch the seams of a boat.

Pintles: the hook-shaped pins on a rudder. They fit into the gudgeons on the stern of the boat, acting as pivots for the rudder.

Plim up: a timber-built boat that has been kept out of the water for any length of time will leak when first used again, owing to the boards having dried and contracted. As the boards swell again on contact with the water, the boat is said to 'plim up'. When fully 'plimmed' it should be quite water-tight.

Poop: the raised stern of a ship; to be swamped by a wave breaking right over the stern.

Port: the left-hand side of a vessel, facing forward. A red navigation light is carried on the port side of a ship at night.

Pram: a small, square-stemmed boat of the dinghy type.

Reach: a stretch of river or navigable channel lying between two bends.

Rubbing strake: the projecting timber which surrounds a boat just below the gunwhale. Its purpose is to prevent damage to the sides of the boat when bumping up against harbour walls, etc.

Sea anchor: a canvas drogue for keeping a boat bows on to the wind when riding out a gale.

Seas: waves.

Seaworthy: in a condition to put to sea.

Shackle: a semi-circular piece of metal, fitted with a screw-in pin, which may be used for joining two pieces of chain, etc.

Sheet: a rope fastened to the corner of a sail in such a way that it may be used for altering the set of the canvas.

Sheet anchor: a large anchor used only in an emergency.

Slip the cable: to cast loose the anchor cable—usually in an emergency without waiting to lift the anchor. A buoy attached to the end of the cable would enable the anchor to be recovered later on.

Starboard: the right-hand side of a boat, facing forward. A green navigation light is carried on the starboard side of a ship at night.

Stays: supports for mast, etc., of wire or rope.

Stem: the timber at the fore end of a boat to which are joined the ends of the boards forming the boat's sides.

Stern: the after part of a boat.

Tack: the course of a boat sailing obliquely to windward.

Tacking: beating to windward on a series of tacks.

Thwarts: the seats for rowers in an open boat.

Trim: to adjust the weight in a boat, so that she rides to her best advantage in the water.

Under way: legally, a boat is 'under way' if not at anchor, made fast to the shore, or aground.

Veer: a shifting of the wind 'with the sun'.

Wake: the disturbed water astern of a moving boat.

Warp: a hauling rope; the act of hauling a boat into a required position by means of a rope, and, possibly, a bollard.

Way: the progress, in any direction, of a boat through the water. (*See also* Headway, Leeway, and Under way.)

Weather: to sail to windward of; to come safely through—i.e. 'to weather a gale'.

Weather Eye Open, Keeping a: to maintain a careful watch when sailing for signs of approaching squalls, etc.

Weather side: the side from which the wind is blowing.

Windward: the direction from which the wind is blowing.

Wreck: a ship destroyed by accident; goods washed ashore from a wrecked ship.

Yaw: the repeated deviation of a boat from an intended course, usually alternatively to port and starboard. Boats will often yaw when being towed if too much weight is placed forward.

BIBLIOGRAPHY

THE information contained in this book has been compiled from many sources: from personal experience; from long shore acquaintances; and from various classes of reading matter—newspaper clippings, magazine articles, books, etc. Those books which I have found most helpful are included in the list given below. Some are now out of print, but most are obtainable through any large public library.

STRANGE CREATURES OF THE TIDE LINE:
A Year at the Shore . . . . . P. H. Gosse
Glaucus . . . . Chas. Kingsley
The Sea-Shore . . . . . . C. M. Yonge
Life of the Shore and Shallow Sea . . . D. P. Wilson
They Live by the Sea . . . . . D. P. Wilson
The Seas . . . . . . F. S. Russell and
                                                    C. M. Yonge
Sea-shore Life of Britain . . . . L. R. Brightwell
Life on the Sea Shore . . . . E. A. R. Ennion

SEA BIRDS:
British Birds in their Haunts . . . . C. A. Johns
The Birds of the British Isles and their Eggs . T. A. Coward
Birds of the Coast . . . . . C. A. G. Hill
Name this Bird . . . . . . E. F. Daglish.
Puffins . . . . . . R. M. Lockley
British Waders in their Haunts . . . S. B. Smith

THE STORY OF THE BOAT:
Ships and Ways of Other Days . . . E. K. Chatterton
Romance of the Sea Rovers . . . . E. K. Chatterton
Tales of the Clipper Ships . . . . C. Fox Smith

SUPERSTITIONS OF THE SEA:
Strange Adventures of the Sea . . . J. G. Lockhart
The Great Iron Ship . . . . . J. Dugan
Windjammers and Shell-backs . . . E. K. Chatterton

BIBLIOGRAPHY

Sea-lore	Stanley Rogers
Ships and Sailors	Stanley Rogers

LIGHTHOUSES AND LIGHTSHIPS:

British Lighthouses, Their History and Romance	J. S. Wryde
British Lighthouses	J. P. Bowen
Trinity House	H. P. Mead
Lighthouse and Lightship . . .	G. W. Phillips
Lightship	A. Binns
Looming Lights	G. G. Carter

THE LIFEBOAT SERVICE:

Modern Motor Lifeboats . . .	J. R. Barnett
Storm on the Waters	C. Vince
The Adventures of the Lifeboat Service .	M. Saville
Wreck—S.O.S.	A. C. Hardy

SMUGGLING:

Smuggling Days and Smuggling Ways . .	Cmdr. H. N. Shore, R.N.
The Smugglers (2 vols.) . . .	Lord Teignmouth (Cmdr. Shore) and Chas. G. Harper
Memoirs of a Smuggler (published at Sidmouth, 1837)	The life story of Jack Rattenbury
The Smugglers of Christchurch, Bourne Heath and the New Forest	E. Russell Oakley
Smuggling in Poole, Bournemouth and Neighbourhood	Bernard C. Short
Compleat Smuggler	J. J. Farjeon
Smuggling Days in Purbeck . . .	W. M. Hardy
Dark Paths	G. Pinnock

TREASURE TROVE:

The Wonders of Salvage	David Masters